The Complete Guide to Shakespeare's Best Plays

Aileen M. Carroll

J. WESTON

WALCH

PUBLISHER

Portland, Maine

User's Guide
to
Walch Reproducible Books

As part of our general effort to provide educational materials that are as practical and economical as possible, we have designated this publication a "reproducible book." The designation means that purchase of the book includes purchase of the right to limited reproduction of all pages on which this symbol appears:

Here is the basic Walch policy: We grant to individual purchasers of this book the right to make sufficient copies of reproducible pages for use by all students of a single teacher. This permission is limited to a single teacher and does not apply to entire schools or school systems, so institutions purchasing the book should pass the permission on to a single teacher. Copying of the book or its parts for resale is prohibited.

Any questions regarding this policy or requests to purchase further reproduction rights should be addressed to:

Permissions Editor
J. Weston Walch, Publisher
321 Valley Street • P.O. Box 658
Portland, Maine 04104-0658

1   2   3   4   5   6   7   8   9   10

ISBN 0-8251-3858-2

Copyright © 1985, 2000
J. Weston Walch, Publisher
P.O. Box 658 • Portland, Maine 04104-0658

Printed in the United States of America

Contents

ROMEO AND JULIET

JULIUS CAESAR

Foreword

This study guide covers six of Shakespeare's best-known plays—among them, the tragedies *Hamlet* and *Macbeth*. Most high school students encounter both of these plays and become interested in them, for although the characters are complex, the story lines are easy enough for the students to follow.

The Roman history play *Julius Caesar* is one that young readers usually find relatively easy to understand because in many cases they already know the circumstances of Caesar's death. Thus, like Shakespeare's original audience, they can concentrate on how he tells the story.

Of the three comedies, *Romeo and Juliet* always appeals to students because it is a tale of teenage rebellion and romance, subjects to which they can easily relate. *A Midsummer Night's Dream* is set in a beautiful fantasy world. Again, it has "love interest" plus broad comedy—a winning combination.

The Tempest, probably Shakespeare's last play, is more difficult. Thus students may need more in-class help with it than with the other comedies. (See "Suggestions for Presenting *The Tempest*," p. 102.) Its examination of good and evil should give rise to some fruitful classroom discussions, while its emphasis on the supernatural and its depiction of "love at first sight" will attract and hold the students' interest.

Since the language of Shakespeare may seem difficult at first, and since neither the poetic nor the dramatic form is as reassuringly familiar as prose, students need some practical advice about how to read a Shakespearean play. That advice can be found in "To the Student." Once the beginning difficulties are behind, young readers generally are caught up in the exciting plot and are eager to read on.

To help explain the intricacies of each plot, a comprehensive act-by-act summary is provided. To prevent students from relying too heavily on those summaries, the reading quizzes contain questions that can only be answered by careful study of the play itself. The lessons for each play emphasize plot, character, setting, and theme; they demand that students reflect and draw conclusions. If students have completed the lessons successfully, the final tests should present no particular difficulties. The supplementary activities suggested for each play are designed to appeal to a variety of students. Some students may want to do a brief oral report. Others, with creative talents, might want to get involved in a longer project.

Both the supplementary activities and the lessons themselves touch upon political and social history. Thus, the study of a Shakespearean play becomes a link to history. References are also made to the Elizabethan fondness for music; the play could be a bridge to that subject, if you choose. Whatever your emphasis, these lessons should help you gain the reward of seeing your students respond to the wisdom and art of William Shakespeare. It is hoped that some of them will be inspired to continue to read and enjoy his work for years to come.

To the Teacher

Lesson Preparation

The six Shakespearean plays most often taught in high school—and treated in this volume—represent varying degrees of reading difficulty. Nevertheless, plot, character, setting, and theme are emphasized in the activities at all levels. Some attention is given to the poetry in each of the plays as well.

You may wish to follow some or all of these suggestions to ensure that your students derive the greatest benefit from their study of the plays:

1. Insist that students keep all act summaries, lessons, quizzes, and tests in a folder or a loose-leaf notebook for easy reference and review. Point out that these materials may also benefit them in their postsecondary work.

2. Make certain that every student reads "To the Student" before reading a play.

3. Use the opening lessons, "Getting Acquainted with Shakespeare" and "A Look at Shakespeare's London," to introduce any of the plays.

4. Point out to the students that although the act summaries are comprehensive, careful reading of the play will be necessary to answer questions on the reading quizzes.

5. Since famous lines from the plays make up part of each final test, you might call students' attention to the most often-quoted lines, either while they are studying the play or before the final test.

6. The lessons for each play demand that students reflect on what they have read and draw conclusions. In a few cases, a general class discussion might be beneficial before students attempt to complete a lesson. The following lessons would be best presented in that manner:

   Romeo and Juliet—Lessons III, IV, VIII; *Julius Caesar*—Lesson XIV; *Macbeth*—Lessons XVI, XVII; *Hamlet*—Lesson XXVIII; *A Midsummer Night's Dream*—

Lessons XXXII, XXXV; *The Tempest*—Lessons XXXVIII, XXXIX, XXXX.

7. Answers for each lesson are included in the Answer Key.

8. When you introduce a play, you might ask students to look at the list of supplementary activities and volunteer for ones that interest them. The vocabulary study would benefit everyone.

Using the Internet

Encourage students to do some independent research based on the suggestions offered for each play. These activities were designed to promote the students' use of their own initiative, creativity, and imagination. Use the Internet as a culminating activity, as an additional way to enrich your students' experience of reading a Shakespearean play.

The following web site is especially useful since it has something to offer students and teachers at various levels.

Mr. William Shakespeare and the Internet
http://daphne.palomar.edu/shakespeare

The site covers such topics as Shakespeare's life and times, his works, the theater, and the Renaissance period. It includes a Shakespeare timeline and even a Shakespeare biography quiz! The site's Shakespeare in Education section is organized around lesson plans and other aides for teaching Shakespeare to high school students, all of which can be tailored to fit your particular class. Mr. William Shakespeare and the Internet offers links to many other Shakespeare-specific web sites designed for both students and teachers.

Additional web sites that may be of use to you or your students are:

The Shakespeare Birthplace Trust
http://www.shakespeare.org.uk

Shakespeare's Globe
http://www.rdg.ac.uk/globe

The Complete Works of William Shakespeare
http://tech-two.mit.edu/Shakespeare/

Name_____ Date_____

To the Student

If you are getting ready to read your first play by William Shakespeare, prepare yourself for a unique and unforgettable reading experience. At first, however, you may have a few difficulties. You must remember that although Shakespeare wrote in modern English, he was using the everyday language of the sixteenth and early seventeenth centuries. Since then, naturally, the English language has changed. If you watch old movies on TV, you may already realize that a mere twenty years can make a difference in our language. With Shakespeare, we are talking about nearly four hundred years!

The following hints will help make your introduction to Shakespeare as painless as possible. Once you get to know him, you will have a friend whose wit and wisdom you can enjoy for life.

1. Before beginning the play, **familiarize yourself with the cast of characters** and their relationships to each other.

2. **Read the footnotes.** They will make the lines of the play much easier for you to understand, will give you definitions of unfamiliar words, and will show you the sense in which a particular word is used. (Quite often, a word may be used in a sense that is not common today.)

3. **Read by punctuation, not by line endings.** Remember that the plays are, for the most part, in poetry (blank verse), and each line must contain a certain number of beats. Thus, the end of a line is not necessarily the end of a sentence.

4. **Read slowly.** Remember that poetry is compressed; that is, ideas are expressed in the fewest possible words. Therefore, each word counts. You must read slowly and know each word in order to make sense of what you read. You will probably need a dictionary for unfamiliar words that are not footnoted.

5. Be like Shakespeare's original audience; **use your imagination.** When he describes a person or place, try to picture that person or place. If you do, the play will certainly "come alive" for you.

6. **Paraphrase the text** in your own words.

William Shakespeare

       The Complete Guide to Shakespeare's Best Plays

Getting Acquainted with Shakespeare

If you could take the ultimate field trip and visit Stratford-on-Avon, Shakespeare's birthplace, you could still find buildings and scenes that were familiar to him. Still standing are the house where he was born; the grammar school he attended; the nearby farmhouse home of Anne Hathaway, his wife; and the fine house and garden of Dr. John Hall, his son-in-law. Perhaps, like other visitors, you'd eat your bag lunch in Dr. Hall's garden, surrounded by flowers that Shakespeare knew and loved. Of course, not all of Stratford is old and quaint; much of it is geared to the thousands of tourists who come each year to see William Shakespeare's birthplace.

But let's try to imagine it as it was in Shakespeare's boyhood, a sixteenth-century English village surrounded by forests where deer wandered freely. Its meadows were dotted with wildflowers, and stately swans sailed along the River Avon. (They still do!) Like the other village lads, Shakespeare wandered through the woods and fields, acquiring early his love and knowledge of nature. That the beauty of the English countryside made a lasting impression on him is shown by his references in the plays to animals, birds, and flowers.

He was born in Stratford, probably on April 23, 1564, and christened on April 26. His father, John Shakespeare, was a prosperous glovemaker who was respected by his neighbors and held various town offices. His mother, Mary Arden, was from a good family and had some fortune, having inherited considerable farm property.

As a young boy, William attended grammar school, where emphasis was on Latin grammar and not much else. Later, in London, he would learn French. For his plays, his reference books would be Ovid's *Metamorphoses* (for mythology), Plutarch's *Lives* (for his Roman history plays), and Holinshed's *Chronicles* (for his English history plays). In his boyhood, traveling players came to Stratford (as they did to Elsinore in *Hamlet)*, introducing him to drama.

By the time William was eighteen, his formal education was long past. He had already assumed a man's responsibilities, marrying in November 1582 Anne Hathaway, eight years his senior. In May 1583, their first child, Susanna, was born. Two years later, Anne gave birth to twins, Hamnet and Judith, christened in February 1585.

Within a year or two, Shakespeare had departed for London to earn fame and fortune, leaving Anne and the family behind. It was not unusual for an actor to have his family with him, even on tours. Anne's failure to join her husband in London seems to indicate that she was a Puritan. Puritans believed that the stage and its actors did much to corrupt people's morals. Actually, a few years later, Puritanism became so strong in London that the theaters were ordered closed. But when Shakespeare arrived there, playgoing was still a popular entertainment, enjoyed and sponsored by Queen Elizabeth herself.

By 1592, Shakespeare was an established actor in London, and he remained an actor throughout his career. His financial success came from his share of the gate (admissions), not from the sale of his plays, which probably netted him only a few pounds each.

His early literary successes were with his narrative poems, *Venus and Adonis* and *The Rape of Lucrece*, both dedicated to his wealthy patron, the young earl of Southampton. In 1594, the theaters reopened after a temporary closing during the plague. From that time, Shakespeare concentrated his literary efforts on plays, producing thirty-seven by the time of his retirement in 1610.

Throughout his career, he was a member of the Lord Chamberlain's Men (later the King's Men), whose leading actor was Richard Burbage. Shakespeare lived quietly and gained a reputation as a polite, good-natured man and a loyal friend. Investing his money wisely, he acquired much property in Stratford, including New Place, to which he eventually retired.

He died there on April 23, 1616. His only son having predeceased him, Shakespeare tried to leave his property intact for a male heir. However, neither daughter produced one. Shakespeare's greatest legacy, his plays, came down to us through the efforts of two actor friends who collected and published them after his death.

Lesson 1: Outlining "Getting Acquainted with Shakespeare" for Ready Reference

1. When and where was Shakespeare born? _____

2. A. What was his father's name and occupation? _____

   B. What was his mother's name? _____

3. How much formal education did Shakespeare have? _____

4. What lasting effect did Stratford and the surrounding countryside have on him? _____

   _____

5. Whom and when did Shakespeare marry? _____

6. What were his children's names? _____

7. Approximately when did he leave Stratford for London? _____

8. Why didn't his wife go with him? _____

9. What was the eventual effect of Puritanism on the theaters? _____

   _____

10. How did Shakespeare become well-to-do? _____

11. What were his earliest literary successes? _____

12. What reference books did he use to write his plays? _____

    _____

13. How many plays did Shakespeare write? _____

14. What was the name of the acting company of which he was a part? _____

    _____

15. What was his reputation in London? _____

16. When did Shakespeare retire, and where did he go? _____

    _____

17. When did he die? _____

A Look at Shakespeare's London

William Shakespeare was a literary genius, probably the greatest that England has produced. It in no way diminishes his greatness to say that Shakespeare was also lucky enough to be in "the right place at the right time."

Consider his arrival in London sometime between 1585 and 1592. His timing couldn't have been better. In 1588, England routed her longtime enemy, Spain, with the defeat of the Spanish Armada. English people took nationalistic pride in that victory, and pride made them eager to know more about their country's history. What pleasanter way to learn history than by watching a drama? As could be expected, Shakespeare's *King Henry VI, Tragedy of King Richard III,* and *Life and Death of King John* played to enthusiastic audiences.

The English were proud, too, of the exploits of such intrepid explorers as Sir Walter Raleigh and Sir Francis Drake, who traveled to the New World and brought back to London reports of riches and savages that sparked everyone's imagination. The city itself had become a leading center of trade. Foreigners of every description thronged its streets. Enterprising teachers offered quick courses in French, Dutch, Italian, and Arabic so Londoners could carry on business with the strangers in their midst. London's diversity enabled a young person with intelligence and a receptive mind to learn much about foreign lands and foreign ways without ever leaving England. Of course, William Shakespeare did just that. He became confident enough of his knowledge of the Continent to set a number of plays in Italy.

To Shakespeare's advantage, too, was the intellectual climate of his day, for England had now entered the Renaissance, which had begun earlier on the Continent. People believed now that they had some freedom of choice, some part in shaping their own destiny. Echoing that belief, Shakespeare wrote in *Julius Caesar,*

> The fault, dear Brutus, is not in our stars,
> But in ourselves, that we are underlings.

In contrast to the Medieval World with its emphasis on the afterlife, the Renaissance offered some rewards here on earth. Science and learning became the pursuits of those fortunate enough to have leisure for them. Eloquence in speech was a sought-after skill; people believed that the use of speech to express thoughts and emotions set man apart from the animals. Shakespeare gives the Renaissance view in Hamlet's famous lines:

> *What a piece of work is man! how noble in reason! how infinite in faculty*! . . . in action how like an angel! in apprehension** how like a god! the beauty of the world! the paragon of animals!*

> *capacity
> **understanding

Of course, Shakespeare himself, with his "apprehension" of human nature, his awareness of the ideas of his era, and his eloquence of expression, was bound to find favor with Elizabethan audiences.

He was fortunate, too, that his plays were enjoyed not only by the "groundlings," who paid a penny apiece to watch, but also by the queen herself. Elizabeth loved the theater. She held firm ideas about both the plays' subjects and presentations, but she was willing to pay for her theatergoing, providing money for costumes and props.

When plays were not presented at court for Elizabeth or her successor, James I (another theater enthusiast), they might be presented in inn yards or—a little later—in theaters such as The Globe, The Theatre, or the Swan. Presentations took place in midafternoon. Boy actors took the female parts. Props were few, although costumes were elaborate. Obviously, the audience needed imagination and Shakespeare's magnificent word pictures to make up for staging deficiencies.

Although sets and lighting were minimal, the actors were so skilled that they made each performance convincing. Their greatest assets were good memories and strong clear voices, but they were also expert fencers, dancers, and even acrobats, and most had good singing voices. Knowing that their audience demanded realism, they often practiced sleight of hand, using retractable knives to simulate stabbings. They wore bladders of sheep's blood under their jackets so that when stabbed, they would bleed copiously. And, in a scene that requiring putting out someone's eye, the actor would allow a grape to fall to the floor at the proper moment.

Actors began training early. Shakespeare, by the standards of his time, came to the profession late. He must have worked exceptionally hard to become a successful actor after only a few years in London. That he was becoming a successful author at the same time is a tribute to his energy and genius.

Lesson 2:
Outlining "Shakespeare's London" for Ready Reference

1. What historic event took place at about the same time as Shakespeare's arrival in London? _____

   _____

2. What effect did that event have on the English people? _____

   _____

3. Why was that effect to Shakespeare's advantage? _____

   _____

4. What advantage was it to the young playwright that England had embarked on an age of explora-

   tion and that London had become a center of trade? _____

   _____

5. How do you suppose Shakespeare gained his knowledge of the French language? _____

   _____

6. How did the Renaissance affect people's viewpoint of destiny or fate? _____

   _____

7. Why did people put so much emphasis on the skillful use of language? _____

   _____

8. What role did Queen Elizabeth and her successor, James I, play in the lives of Shakespeare and his

   fellow actors? _____

   _____

9 Name three early theaters. _____

   _____

10. Name three ways in which the presentation of plays in Elizabethan times differed from the

    presentation of plays today. _____

    _____

11. List at least five requirements for Elizabethan actors. _____

    _____

    _____

To the Teacher:

Suggestions for Presenting *Romeo and Juliet*

Sources for the Play

Students are generally surprised to learn that Shakespeare's plots were not his own, but were based on earlier stories. His original audience would have known how the play would end, but they were interested in the playwright's choice of words to tell the story.

Romeo and Juliet, for example, dates back to a Greek story of the fifth century A.D. In that version, a woman, to avoid an arranged marriage, takes a drug that causes her to fall into a deathlike sleep. A fifteenth-century Italian version is very similar except that Juliet, in that account, retires to a nunnery and dies there. A sixteenth-century retelling was published in Venice, but the action, as in Shakespeare's play, takes place in Verona. Finally, an English poet, Arthur Brooke, wrote the Romeo and Juliet story in rhyming couplets (two consecutive lines that rhyme). It seems likely that Shakespeare read Brooke's poem and then improved on it. Today, directors faced with the production of a Shakespearean play may choose to have the actors in modern dress and the setting contemporary as well. Thus, each retelling creates a slightly different effect, but Shakespeare's language remains unsurpassed.

Topics for Class Discussion

As a group activity, ask students to list on the chalkboard the ways in which Romeo and Juliet are both less and more restricted than young people of their age today. Remind them that Juliet is about to be fourteen and Romeo is not much older.

Have a group of students watch a video of a movie version of *Romeo and Juliet.* Have them answer such questions as, "How does the movie compare with the original play?" Ask them which they prefer, and why. Other class members could also ask them questions such as, "How were the leading characters portrayed in the movie?"

Topics for Oral Reports

Have some students read the modern play *West Side Story* and report to the class the ways in which it is like and unlike *Romeo and Juliet.*

Remind students that Shakespeare was a country man, familiar with the fields and forests of his native Stratford, and that references to herbs and flowers are numerous in his plays. Ask for volunteers to consult an herbal (a book about herbs and other plants) and report on the supposed medicinal and magical properties of the herbs mentioned in *Romeo and Juliet*—for example, fennel, plantain, wormwood, and rosemary. (Two good references are *Shakespeare's Flowers* by Jessica Kerr and Culpepper's *Complete Herbal.*)

Hands-On Activities

Ask a group of students to try to find pictures of all the flowers mentioned in *Romeo and Juliet.* Have them mount the pictures as a collage for the class bulletin board. See especially fennel (Act I, Scene II, line 29); rosemary (Act III, Scene IV, line 213); rose (Act II, Scene II, line 43); and wormwood (Act I, Scene III, line 26).

Ask a group of students to make a collage or do sketches of their impressions of Romeo and Juliet.

Suggest that some students look for newspaper ads for Shakespeare's plays or find magazine articles about him. (Introduce them to the *Reader's Guide to Periodical Literature.*) They can then mount the materials they find and make a bulletin board display. This exercise will help students to become aware that Shakespeare's plays are still very popular.

Vocabulary Building

Ask each student to collect in a notebook at least two unfamiliar words from each scene of the play, avoiding words that are footnoted. They should then look up each word, define it, and write a sentence using it. In class, students can compare notes and learn from one another's work.

What Happens in Act I, *Romeo and Juliet*

Act I, Scene I On a street in Verona, Italy, Sampson and Gregory, two servants of the Capulets, are joking in puns. Abram and Balthasar, servants of the Capulets' enemies, the Montagues, appear and Sampson and Gregory provoke them to a sword fight. Benvolio, a member of the Montague family, comes along and tells the servants to stop fighting. He, in turn, is challenged by Tybalt, a quick-tempered member of the Capulet family. An officer stops their swordplay as old Capulet and his wife appear. Capulet is ready to fight and challenges old Montague, who comes along at the same moment with his wife. The two wives try vainly to stop the old men, but it takes the Prince of Verona, who is next on the scene, to quiet them. He does so by threatening death if they disturb the peace once more.

With peace restored, Montague and his wife talk with their nephew, Benvolio. They express concern about their son, Romeo, who is melancholy and who wanders alone in the early morning, returning home to sleep all day. As they part, Benvolio promises his aunt and uncle that he will talk to Romeo and discover what is making him troubled and restless. Romeo appears, and Benvolio questions him. Romeo talks generally of love, then confesses that he loves a girl who apparently has no interest in him or in marriage. Benvolio's advice is to find another girl, but Romeo is certain he could love no other.

Act I, Scene II On a street, old Capulet is talking with Count Paris, who wants to marry Capulet's nearly-fourteen-year-old daughter, Juliet. Capulet does not actually discourage the suit, but says that she is his only living child and is still very young. He suggests that Paris wait two years. If his daughter is willing, he will then give his consent to the marriage. He invites Paris to a large party he is giving that evening and sends his servant out with a list of other guests to invite. The poor servant, not being able to read, asks the first gentlemen he meets (Benvolio and Romeo) to read the list for him. They do, and decide to appear at the Capulets' party, for Rosaline, the girl Romeo loves in vain, will be there. Romeo wants to worship her from afar, but Benvolio wants him to compare her with all the other beautiful women who will attend. He thinks that Romeo may then find Rosaline not quite as desirable as he had thought.

Act I, Scene III Lady Capulet is talking about her daughter, Juliet, to Juliet's nurse, a talkative old woman. Lady Capulet asks the nurse to call Juliet. When she comes, Lady Capulet tells the girl about Paris's proposal of marriage. She tells Juliet that Paris will be at their party and that she will have a chance to see how handsome he is. Juliet seems completely obedient to her mother's wish that she become interested in Paris.

Act I, Scene IV Masked, Romeo, Benvolio, and Mercutio (Romeo's friend) are on their way to the Capulet party. Benvolio says that they will stay for one dance only. Romeo claims his heart is too heavy; he will not dance. Mercutio teases him and tries to cheer him, but Romeo has a sense of dread about the night's activities.

Act I, Scene V The Capulets' servingmen are joking together. Then the Capulets, Juliet and her nurse, and Tybalt greet their masked guests. The young people dance while Capulet and a relative talk about their own youth. Romeo, who has come in with the other maskers, sees Juliet for the first time and is struck by her beauty. When Romeo speaks, Tybalt recognizes him as a Montague and is about to attack him, but old Capulet intervenes. He recognizes Romeo too, but says mildly that the boy is well spoken of in Verona and that Tybalt must not spoil the evening by any show of ill will.

Meanwhile, Romeo approaches Juliet. She is as charmed with him as he is with her. They talk as lovers, then kiss. The nurse comes to tell Juliet that her mother wants to talk with her, and Romeo then realizes he has been talking of love to the daughter of the Capulets. Benvolio suggests that it is time to leave, but Capulet hospitably urges them to stay for the supper. They do leave, however. Meanwhile, Juliet quizzes her nurse about Romeo. When she finds that she has fallen in love with the son of her family's great enemy, she, like Romeo, is very troubled.

Name _____ Date _____

Lesson 3: Getting Acquainted with the Characters

To understand a play, you must be able to follow the action (the plot). So far, in *Romeo and Juliet,* the plot has been outlined for you in the summary of Act I. You must also be able to see in your mind the setting (when and where the action takes place). In Act I, Shakespeare gives you only a few details of the setting. So far, the story takes place in Verona, Italy, on the street or in the house of the well-to-do Capulets. Above all, you must get acquainted with the characters. Imagine how they look. Observe the ways they behave. Try to under-stand their reasons for behaving as they do as you listen in on their conversations and get to know their thoughts, which they reveal in soliloquies. (**A soliloquy** is a speech made by an actor who is alone on the stage, thinking aloud.)

To test your understanding of the characters so far, match each character below with the adjective or adjectives that best describe him or her. Some adjectives may apply to more than one person.

1.   A.   Montague _____
     B.   Capulet _____
     C.   Romeo _____
     D.   Mercutio _____
     E.   Benvolio _____
     F.   Tybalt _____
     G.   Lady Capulet _____
     H.   Nurse _____
     I.   Paris _____
     J.   Juliet _____
     K.   the Prince _____

lovesick
melancholy
lighthearted
sensible
peaceable
hotheaded
matter-of-fact
talkative
beautiful
wealthy
handsome
just
hospitable
easily angered
bawdy

2. Was Romeo truly in love with Rosaline? Explain. _____

_____

3. What evidence do you have that Benvolio is more practical and worldly than Romeo? (Clue: Remember his advice to Romeo.) _____

_____

4. In recommending Count Paris to her daughter, what quality or qualities of his does Lady Capulet emphasize? What does this reveal about her values? _____

_____

Now one question about the plot:

5. The servants in the opening scene, the servants in the Capulet house before the party, and Juliet's nurse all add humor to the opening act. Are there any indications, though, that this play is not a comedy? Explain.

_____

_____

        The Complete Guide to Shakespeare's Best Plays

Reading Quiz: *Romeo and Juliet,* Act I

1. What indications are there that the feud between the Montagues and Capulets has been going on for some time?

   _____

   _____

2. When Benvolio saw Romeo at dawn, what did Romeo do?

   _____

   _____

3. Why is it possible for Romeo and his friends to enter the Capulet house and mingle with the guests, undetected, until Tybalt recognizes Romeo's voice?

   _____

   _____

4. When Lady Capulet mentions Count Paris to Juliet, what is the nurse's reaction?

   _____

   _____

5. Approximately how long is it since old Capulet himself has danced at a ball? What indication was there in an earlier scene that Lady Capulet is considerably younger than her husband?

   _____

   _____

What Happens in Act II, *Romeo and Juliet*

Act II, Scene I After the Capulet party, Romeo slips away from Benvolio and Mercutio and returns to the Capulet orchard (garden). Benvolio and Mercutio come calling and hunting for him. They soon give up, deciding that Romeo does not want to be found.

Act II, Scene II Alone now in the orchard, Romeo sees Juliet at her window and, in a poetic soliloquy, praises her beauty. He hears Juliet start to speak, repeating his name and expressing sorrow that it is Montague. Finally, she tells herself that it is the name only that is her enemy; without it, Romeo could have all her love. Romeo answers her, saying that for her love, he would give up his name. Juliet is startled to hear his voice and is alarmed for his safety, should any of her kinsmen find him, but Romeo is indifferent to his danger. Juliet then worries that Romeo will think her "too quickly won" since she has already expressed her love. Romeo then vows his love for her, but she is concerned that things are happening too quickly. When her nurse calls from inside the house, Juliet leaves Romeo briefly. She returns to say good night and to tell Romeo that she will send a messenger to him the next day. If Romeo is sincere, he can tell the messenger when and where Juliet can meet him to be married; if he is not sincere, she begs him to leave her to her misery. After his reassurance and a tender good night, Juliet retires. Romeo goes to see his confessor, Friar Lawrence, and tells him the good news.

Act II, Scene III It is dawn now, and Friar Lawrence is going out to gather medicinal herbs as Romeo appears. The friar guesses that either Romeo is very troubled and cannot sleep or he has been up all night. Romeo admits happily that he has not been to bed. He asks the friar to marry him to Juliet Capulet that very day. Friar

Sir Ian McKellen as Romeo

Lawrence reminds Romeo how recent it was that he was pining for Rosaline. The old man realizes that Romeo was actually more in love with the idea of love than he ever was with Rosaline. He agrees to marry him to Juliet, hoping the marriage will end the Montague-Capulet feud.

Act II, Scene IV In a street, Mercutio and Benvolio are talking about Romeo's not having returned home the previous night. Benvolio says that Tybalt has sent a letter to Romeo's house, challenging him to a duel. Jokingly, Mercutio says that Romeo is already dead for love, and now he will face a deadly enemy. When Romeo appears, Mercutio teases him about giving them the slip the previous night, and he and Romeo continue to pun. At that point, Juliet's nurse and her servant, Peter, appear. Mercutio teases the nurse a little, as he does everyone. When he and Benvolio leave, the nurse scolds her servant for allowing Mercutio to be saucy to her. She then tells Romeo whose messenger she is and warns him to be gentlemanly to her Juliet. Romeo tells her that Juliet should go that afternoon to Friar Lawrence for confession and forgiveness. There she and Romeo will be married. Romeo arranges for the nurse to meet his servant and take home a rope ladder, which will be his means of getting into Juliet's room that night.

Act II, Scene V Juliet has been waiting three hours for the nurse's return, and when the old lady comes, she is slow to deliver the message. Finally, she comes to the point and tells Juliet to go to Friar Lawrence's cell on the pretext of going to confession. Meanwhile, the nurse will pick up the rope ladder.

Act II, Scene VI Romeo and Friar Lawrence are waiting for Juliet. Prophetically, Romeo says that once the marriage is performed, let "love-devouring death do what he dare," they will have each other. Friar Lawrence counsels moderation, saying that too much emotion may destroy the love that inspired it. Juliet arrives, and she and Romeo talk of their love. The friar marries them immediately.

Lesson 4: Three Character Studies

Although *Romeo and Juliet* is a tragedy, that fact is not immediately apparent. The first two acts contain quite a bit of humor, some provided by the servants, as you have already noted, but much stemming from the speeches of Juliet's nurse and Romeo's friend, Mercutio. Of course, their humor differs as much as their characters and their stations in life. The nurse's humor is bawdy, filled with crude sexual references. Mercutio can be bawdy, but his humor is generally clever and imaginative and is filled with plays on words. Aside from their humor, both the nurse and Mercutio are memorable in other ways. Let's examine their speeches to see what is revealed about their characters.

1. First, reread in Act I, Scene III, lines 75–76 and 78, the nurse's praise of Paris. Now, in Act II, Scene V, lines 38–46 and 56–58, see her comments on Romeo. What do you conclude about the nurse as a judge of men? What do you conclude about her loyalty?

   _____

2. In Act I, Scene III, you met the nurse for the first time. Reread her speeches prompted by Lady Capulet's simple statement that Juliet is "not fourteen" yet. What characteristic of the nurse do these speeches show?

   _____

3. What indication do you have that the nurse is sincerely fond of Juliet?

   _____

4. Do you think the nurse is completely loyal to her employers, the Capulets? Explain.

   _____

5. Now look first at Mercutio's speech in Act I, Scene IV, beginning with line 53, and his speech in the same scene, beginning with line 96. How do these speeches show him as an imaginative, well-educated man of the world?

   _____

6. Reread his speeches in Act II, Scene I and in Act II, Scene IV, lines 13–17, 39–48, and 92–97. Would you say that Mercutio views falling in love with the same seriousness that Romeo does? Explain.

   _____

7. Mercutio's comments to and about the nurse are disrespectful (Act II, Scene IV). What judgment do you think he has made about her character?

   _____

8. Friar Lawrence is a holy man, a wise man, and a practical man. Reread his opening speech in Act II, Scene III as he is about to go gather herbs. In lines 9–10, he states a paradox (an apparent contradiction that actually reveals a truth). What is the idea he expresses?

   _____

9. Now look at lines 17–18 in the same speech and restate the idea.

   _____

10. From his comments to Romeo in this scene and from his closing comment in Scene VI, what indications are there that the friar is a practical man with a good understanding of human nature?

   _____

11. What advice to Romeo (which Friar Lawrence states more than once) is in the following brief speech? "Wisely and slow. They stumble that run fast."

   _____

Reading Quiz: *Romeo and Juliet,* Act II

1. How does Romeo reply when the friar asks him if he has spent the night with Rosaline?

   _____

   _____

2. What do Benvolio and Mercutio think is the explanation for Romeo's not having come home the previous night?

   _____

   _____

3. According to the nurse's comment to Romeo, what is Juliet's attitude toward Count Paris?

   _____

   _____

4. Why doesn't the nurse tell Juliet immediately what Romeo's message was?

   _____

   _____

5. Why is it possible for Juliet to leave the house alone to meet Romeo?

   _____

   _____

What Happens in Act III, *Romeo and Juliet*

Act III, Scene I In a public place, Benvolio suggests to Mercutio that they go home; the day is hot, and there is a good chance that they might meet the Capulets and get into a fight. Mercutio teases peaceable Benvolio, accusing him of being ever quick to fight. Tybalt comes along, ready to give or take offense, as always. Mercutio begins to bait him, while Benvolio, concerned that there might be a fight, begs them to withdraw to a more private place. Romeo appears. Tybalt calls him "villain," but Romeo tries to calm Tybalt, not wishing to fight with Juliet's cousin. Mistaking Romeo's gentleness for submission, Mercutio decides to fight Tybalt himself. They fight; Romeo tries to separate them, and as he does, Tybalt gives Mercutio a fatal thrust, then runs off. Mercutio, knowing he is dying, asks Benvolio to help him to a nearby house. Left alone, Romeo is greatly troubled that his friend has been mortally wounded trying to defend Romeo's honor. Romeo, in turn, has allowed Tybalt to insult him because, for Juliet's sake, he would not fight. Benvolio returns to say that Mercutio is dead, and Romeo knows that more trouble is to come. Tybalt reappears. Romeo, angry now, is ready to avenge Mercutio's death. They fight, and Tybalt is killed. Benvolio urges Romeo to flee the prince's wrath and the citizens' fury. He does. The prince, the Montagues, the Capulets, and citizens come in. Benvolio gives a truthful account of the events, but Lady Capulet doubts him because he is related to the Montagues. The prince's decision is that Romeo immediately go into exile or face death.

Act III, Scene II Juliet, alone, is impatient for the night, which will bring her Romeo. The nurse arrives with the news of Tybalt's death, but she is so long in telling it that Juliet at first thinks Romeo is dead. Finally, she realizes that Tybalt was killed by Romeo and Romeo now is banished. The nurse promises Juliet that Romeo will be with her that night. She goes to talk to him at Friar Lawrence's cell, taking a ring of Juliet's as a token of faith.

Act III, Scene III Friar Lawrence brings Romeo the news that the prince has banished him for killing Tybalt. Romeo sees banishment as worse than death. Before the friar can calm him, the nurse arrives. Romeo begs for news of Juliet, then, assuming his beloved must hate him now, threatens to kill himself. The friar chides him, pointing out that the situation is not hopeless. He tells Romeo to go to Juliet that night, but to leave early in the morning before the watchmen make their rounds.

Act III, Scene IV Paris has come to the Capulets' house. Juliet's father has promised him that he and Juliet will be married the following Thursday (quietly, of course, out of respect for Tybalt). Capulet tells his wife to inform Juliet.

Act III, Scene V It is dawn, and Romeo and Juliet know they must part. The nurse comes in to warn Juliet that her mother is coming. Romeo says a sorrowful farewell to Juliet. Lady Capulet comes in, still vowing revenge on Romeo, and tells Juliet that her father has arranged for her to marry Paris the following Thursday. Juliet refuses, saying that she will not marry yet. Lady Capulet becomes very angry, and at that moment, her husband and the nurse arrive. When Lady Capulet tells him that Juliet refuses to marry, he storms about and is so abusive to Juliet that his wife tries to calm him. He threatens to throw Juliet out of the house if she refuses to marry Paris. Juliet appeals to her mother in vain. When her parents leave, she appeals to the nurse, whose only advice is that she marry Paris since Romeo is as good as dead. Juliet resolves to go to talk to Friar Lawrence, now her only friend.

12 *The Complete Guide to Shakespeare's Best Plays*

Lesson 5: Some Points Worth Considering

In Lesson 4 it was pointed out that the first two acts of *Romeo and Juliet* contain much humor. If you read carefully, however, these acts also contain **foreshadowings** (indications of what is to come) of tragedy.

1. Look again, for example, at Juliet's speech in Act II, Scene II, lines 116–120. Why is she uneasy?

   _____

2. See Romeo's speech in Act II, Scene VI, lines 3–8. What indication is there that he fears his time with Juliet will be brief?

   _____

In Act III, with the death of lighthearted Mercutio and Romeo's killing of Tybalt, the tragic sequence of events has begun, and the action becomes very fast. Within twenty-four hours after Romeo and Juliet's marriage, Mercutio and Tybalt die; Romeo is banished; Capulet promises Juliet to Count Paris; and Juliet, heartsick, goes to Friar Lawrence for help. Certainly, the emphasis in this act is on plot, but you can find some interesting sidelights on character in the following:

3. Review old Capulet's first discussion with Paris about his marrying Juliet in Act I, Scene II. Under what two conditions will the father consent to Paris's marrying his daughter?

   _____

4. Now look at Capulet's conversation with Paris in Act III, Scene IV. How has Capulet's attitude toward the marriage changed? Why has it changed?

   _____

5. In Act III, Scene V, when Capulet insists that Juliet marry Paris, how is his attitude different from that in Act I, Scene II? Why is he so harsh with Juliet?

   _____

6. Both Friar Lawrence and the nurse give their support to Romeo and Juliet and make their marriage possible. What reasons does the friar have for helping them? Clue: See Act II, Scene IV, lines 90–93 and Act II, Scene VI, lines 36–37. What do you think is the nurse's reason for helping them? In your opinion, who has the better reasons, Friar Lawrence or the nurse?

   _____

   _____

7. In Act III, Scene I, line 138, Romeo calls himself "Fortune's fool." In other words, Fortune or Fate is using him like a plaything; he has no control of his own life. In each of the following instances, is he "Fortune's fool," or is he responsible for what happens? Explain.

   A. his attending the Capulet party _____

   B. his falling in love with Juliet _____

   C. his marrying Juliet _____

   D. his killing Tybalt _____

Reading Quiz: *Romeo and Juliet,* **Act III**

1. Why does Mercutio hold Romeo partly responsible for the wound Tybalt gave him?

   _____

2. What does the nurse bring with her when she comes to tell Juliet of Tybalt's death?

   _____

3. What is Juliet's first reaction when she hears that Romeo has slain Tybalt?

   _____

4. To what city is Romeo exiled?

   _____

5. What is Friar Lawrence's plan for Romeo in exile?

   _____

6. When Romeo attempts to stab himself, what does the friar accuse him of?

   _____

7. How does Lady Capulet plan to take revenge on Romeo in exile?

   _____

8. At the end of Act III, what does Juliet say she will do if all else fails?

   _____

What Happens in Act IV, *Romeo And Juliet*

Act IV, Scene I Paris has come to Friar Lawrence to arrange his marriage to Juliet. When Friar Lawrence tries to delay, Paris explains that Juliet's father thinks she should marry immediately because she is grieving and too much alone. Juliet appears, and Paris speaks to her lovingly as his future wife. Juliet's words to him have a double meaning, significant to the audience. Paris leaves her alone with her confessor. She then tells Friar Lawrence that she will kill herself rather than marry Paris. The friar suggests a plan that will take great courage on her part. He will give her an herb that will put her into a deathlike coma. Her parents, believing her to be dead, will place her body in the Capulet tomb. Friar Lawrence and Romeo will be there when she awakes, and Romeo will take her off to Mantua.

Act IV, Scene II Capulet is making preparations for the wedding when Juliet returns, seemingly remorseful that she was disobedient and now willing to marry Paris. Old Capulet is delighted at the change in his daughter, gives the friar credit for it, and goes off to tell Count Paris about her positive attitude.

Act IV, Scene III Giving clever excuses, Juliet convinces both her mother and the nurse to leave her alone. Despite terrible misgivings, she takes Friar Lawrence's potion.

Act IV, Scene IV It is late at night, and the Capulets, with the nurse, are still urging the servants to complete the cooking for the wedding. The nurse tells old Capulet to go to bed, saying he will be sick the next day if he doesn't. He, however, continues to supervise preparations. He hears music, knows the bridegroom is approaching, and sends the nurse to wake Juliet.

Act IV, Scene V The nurse tries to wake Juliet, thinking that she is sleeping soundly. When she draws the curtains aside and sees Juliet stretched out on the bed, fully clothed, she assumes Juliet is dead and cries wildly for help. Both parents come in and are so stunned by the sight of their daughter that they are powerless to do anything. Next, the friar, Paris, and the musicians come in. Amid the laments that follow, Friar Lawrence points out that Juliet, dying young, has gone to Heaven; they must remember that, even though they grieve. Capulet says sadly that all their wedding preparations have turned to funeral preparations. Friar Lawrence preaches acceptance, saying that Heaven has punished them for some reason but that they must accept what has happened.

When the principals leave the stage, Peter and the musicians exchange lively banter, and the musicians decide to stay for their dinner anyway, even though the wedding has become a funeral.

Romeo and Juliet in Friar Lawrence's cell

Name _____ Date _____

Lesson 6: Shakespeare's Language

In Shakespeare's day, Londoners were having a love affair with their language. Everyone from the queen's courtiers (attendants) to the "groundlings" who paid a penny apiece to see a performance appreciated the witty conversations, the clever plays on words, and the poetic phrases that filled Shakespeare's plays.

Romeo and Juliet is no exception. To illustrate, let's look first at Juliet's conversation with Paris in Friar Lawrence's cell. Remember that she is nervous, yet her replies to Paris are clever and filled with double meanings that the audience would have understood and enjoyed.

1. For example, see Act IV, Scene I, line 19, when she replies to Paris, "That may be, sir, when I may be a wife." How would Paris have interpreted her meaning?

   _____

   How would the audience have interpreted it?

   _____

2. Witty word play was not restricted to the upper classes in the play. See Peter's conversation with the musicians (Act IV, Scene V) and their variations on the phrase *silver sound*. In what different senses do they use it?

   _____

3. Finally, reread Mercutio's description of Queen Mab and her carriage and servants in Act I, Scene IV, lines 54–69. List the details Mercutio (Shakespeare) gives, poetic phrases that make the description vivid for both the reader and the audience.

   _____

4. Now from the entire speech, lines 53–54, list all the words that are unfamiliar to you. Look them up in a dictionary if they are not footnoted. Don't be discouraged if your list seems long; Shakespeare's vocabulary was remarkable. His plays contain nearly 18,000 different words.

   _____

If you had difficulty in reading some parts of the play, you may have the impression that Shakespeare was too "literary" and used too many long words. Actually, he used the popular speech of his day and even used slang. Part of your problem may be that his vocabulary was so extensive or that he used words that are now out of date.

5. The following words appear in the play and were commonly used in Shakespeare's time. Define each word, using a dictionary if necessary:

   Sirrah_____Coz _____ Wast _____

   Mine, as in "Mine eye" _____ Thee _____

6. All the following words were taken from Acts I and II. Complete each sentence with the correct word. You may need to look up some of the words in a dictionary.

   misadventure, fray, beseeches, inconstant, nuptial, disparagement

   A. What was to have been Juliet's _____ feast became her funeral feast.

   B. Tybalt's _____ of Romeo so angered Mercutio that he took out his sword against Tybalt.

   C. At first, Romeo seems _____ in his affections. He supposedly loves Rosaline, yet he falls in love with Juliet at first sight.

   D. Romeo _____ Friar Lawrence to marry him to Juliet.

   E. It was a _____ that brought Mercutio and Benvolio to the same place as Tybalt.

   F. When Romeo stepped into the _____, he accidentally gave Tybalt a chance to slay Mercutio.

What Happens in Act V, *Romeo and Juliet*

Act V, Scene I Romeo, now in Mantua, has had a happy dream and is in good spirits when his servant appears. Romeo asks eagerly for news of Juliet. Balthasar tells him that Juliet is dead; he himself has seen her placed in the Capulet tomb. Against Balthasar's advice, Romeo decides to return to Verona. From a poor apothecary (druggist), he buys a deadly poison and rides wildly back to Verona.

Act V, Scene II Friar John, who was to have carried Friar Lawrence's message advising Romeo to be at the Capulet tomb at a designated hour, returns to Friar Lawrence's cell. He explains that he was prevented from delivering the message. Friar Lawrence goes immediately to the Capulet tomb so he will be on hand when Juliet awakes. He plans to take her home with him until he can get another letter to Romeo.

Act V, Scene III Paris, who has gone to Juliet's tomb to scatter flowers, sees Romeo arrive. Romeo's servant carries a light and tools to open the door of the tomb. Thinking that Romeo intends to desecrate the dead, Paris challenges him. Romeo does not want to harm Paris and urges him to leave, but Paris will not. They fight, and Paris is mortally wounded. Dying, he asks Romeo to place his body near Juliet's. Romeo does so. In a soliloquy, Romeo talks to his supposedly dead Juliet. He then takes the poison he brought and collapses beside her. Friar Lawrence arrives and learns from Balthasar, who has remained close by, that Romeo has been in the tomb for half an hour. Friar Lawrence approaches the tomb alone and sees the bloody swords. He goes in to find both Paris and Romeo dead and Juliet just beginning to wake.

Juliet sits up, sees the friar and asks immediately for Romeo. Friar Lawrence has heard a noise. He begs Juliet to leave quickly with him, for her Romeo is dead. Juliet refuses. When she is alone with Romeo's body, she notices the poison cup still in his hand and wishes that there was some left for her. Just then, she hears the watchmen approaching, and seizing Romeo's dagger, she stabs herself to death.

The chief watchman finds Paris and Juliet, newly dead, "who hath here lain this two days buried." He sends his deputies to notify the prince, the Montagues, and the Capulets. The watchmen soon find both Romeo's servant and the friar and bring them back to be held for the prince's arrival. When the prince and the Capulets arrive, old Capulet sees Romeo's dagger in Juliet's breast. Montague arrives and sees his dead son.

The prince is about to begin an investigation when Friar Lawrence steps forward to tell his story. He tells about marrying Romeo and Juliet on the very day that Tybalt was slain; of Juliet's desperation when her parents were forcing her to marry someone else; of the potion he gave her to put her into a deathlike sleep; of his letter to Romeo that never was delivered; of his own arrival at the tomb for Juliet's awakening, only to find both Paris and Romeo dead; and finally, of his entreaty to Juliet to go with him and of her refusal and suicide.

From their servants, the prince then gets an explanation of how Paris and Romeo came to be at the tomb. The prince reads the letter that Romeo had given Balthasar to deliver to his parents, telling of buying the poison and coming to die with his Juliet. The prince blames the senseless Montague-Capulet feud for the tragedies and blames himself that he did not take firmer measures to end it. Montague and Capulet, united in sorrow, forget their differences. Each vows to erect a monument in honor of the other's child.

Name _____ Date _____

Lesson 7: Shakespeare's Poetry

You may not have realized that Shakespeare's plays are written in a poetic form called **blank verse**. Of course, not every single line is poetry. In Act I, Scene II, lines 38–45, the Capulet servant speaks in prose, as we do in any conversation. It is important, though, that you know what blank verse is so you can appreciate the skill required to compose line after line of it, making it seem as natural as ordinary speech. Simply stated, a line of blank verse has five divisions or, to use a musical term, **measures**. Each measure (or **foot**, as it is called in poetry) is made up of two syllables, with the accent always on the second syllable. This line of Juliet's to Romeo (Act II, Scene II, line 134) illustrates:

My love / as deep;/ the more / I give / to thee
  1   2   3   4   5

Read the line, emphasizing the accented syllables, and you will begin to sense the rhythm of blank verse. Now try reading several lines in the play, accenting each second syllable. You have now become aware of blank verse. By definition, one line of blank verse does not rhyme with another. Shakespeare occasionally does rhyme his lines, especially at the end of a scene. For example, in the closing lines of Act I, Scene II, Romeo says,

I'll go along, no such sight to be shown,
But to rejoice in splendor of mine own.

1. Now divide each of the closing lines above into five feet and mark each accented syllable. Some scholars believe that Shakespeare used rhyme to close a scene because actors waiting in the wings could learn or hear a rhymed line more easily and would be ready to make their appearance on cue.

Shakespeare regularly used metaphors, similes, and allusions in his poetry. All these devices make his descriptions more vivid. Let's review the definitions of these literary devices. A **metaphor** is a comparison of two unlike things that have one feature in common. *Example:* "My mind to me a kingdom is."

2. In the above metaphor, what is compared to what? In what sense is the first like the second?

_____

A **simile** is also a comparison. It differs from a metaphor only in that a simile points out the comparison by using *like* or *as. Example:* Agnes runs like a deer.

3. In the above simile, what is implied or suggested about Agnes's running ability?

_____

An **allusion** is a reference to history or literature in order to make a comparison. *Example:* Jason has the strength of Hercules.

4. How strong is Jason? _____

By using metaphors, similes, and allusions, a writer can say a great deal in a small space. These devices are especially useful to a poet, for poetry is, by nature, compressed.

5. Finally, look at some lines from *Romeo and Juliet*. Label A, B, and C as metaphor, simile, or allusion. Then state what is implied by each comparison.

A. Act I, Scene I, lines 215–216:   *She'll not be hit*
                                 With Cupid's arrow. She hath Dian's wit, _____

B. Act I, Scene V, lines 47–48:   . . . . *she hangs upon the cheek of night*
                                 Like a rich jewel in an Ethiop's ear— _____

C. Act II, Scene II, line 3: *It is the East, and Juliet is the sun!* _____

Reading Quiz: *Romeo and Juliet,* **Acts IV and V**

1. After taking Friar Lawrence's potion, how long will Juliet sleep?

   _____

2. As Juliet is about to take the potion that will put her into a coma, what dreadful suspicion of Friar Lawrence goes through her mind?

   _____

3. Why couldn't Friar John deliver Friar Lawrence's letter to Romeo?

   _____

4. What is Paris's page supposed to do while his master is at Juliet's tomb?

   _____

5. Before going into the tomb, what does Romeo instruct his servant Balthasar to do?

   _____

6. When old Montague comes to the Capulet tomb, what does he say has happened to his wife?

   _____

7. What final good came from the deaths of Romeo and Juliet?

   _____

Name _____ Date _____

Lesson 8: Examining the Themes in *Romeo and Juliet*

As you may already know, William Shakespeare is the most famous playwright the world has ever produced. You may be curious about why this is so.

Most of Shakespeare's plots were not original, and his audience knew in advance how the story would "turn out." His characters were remarkable because he understood human nature so well, and his choice of words and his poetry have been admired in every generation.

Aside from his ability to create unforgettable characters and to use the English language with great skill, Shakespeare presented themes or universal ideas that are as true today as they were when he wrote the plays. That is why his comedies and tragedies have lived on.

Students sometimes have difficulties with the notion of theme; often, they confuse it with plot. The **theme** is the central idea of a piece of literature. If the play or novel is complicated, it may have a central theme and several less important themes. Let's examine the idea of theme first in a type of writing with which many of you are famil-iar, the teenage novel. In these novels, a popular theme is "The course of true love never did run smooth." (By the way, that is a quotation from Shakespeare's *A Midsummer Night's Dream*.) The **plot** of such a novel might be summarized like this: John meets Mary. They fall in love. Their families object to their "going steady" or getting married because they are so young. Then a series of problems occurs—perhaps the young people are separated, or perhaps one develops a serious illness, and the other faces this situation with a maturity that surprises the parents. If the story has the traditional happy ending, the young people's love is so strong that they overcome all obstacles and are finally free to marry. This example shows that the theme is illustrated by incidents in the plot or main story of a literary work.

Incidentally, part of the above plot summary could apply to Romeo and Juliet, but the play does not have the traditional happy ending.

Let's take a moment now to look at some possible themes in *Romeo and Juliet*.

1. "The course of true love never did run smooth." Explain in the fewest possible words how the play illustrates this theme.

   _____

   _____

2. Violence begets, or brings about, more violence. Again, explain how this theme is illustrated in *Romeo and Juliet*, using incidents from the play.

   _____

   _____

3. In life, as in love affairs, moderation is the best policy. As you look for incidents that illustrate this theme, remember that Juliet herself thought things were moving too fast and that Friar Lawrence advised moderation. Try to imagine how the story might have turned out if the young people had not married so hastily.

   _____

   _____

4. Disobedience to recognized authority inevitably brings retribution (punishment). Whether or not you agree with this statement, Shakespeare's audience would have expected that Romeo and Juliet were bound to bring trouble and punishment upon themselves by marrying secretly, knowing their parents would object. How is this theme illustrated in the play?

   _____

   _____

In thinking about these questions, you may have begun to realize why Shakespeare's plays continue to interest people. Each generation finds in them ideas that are still pertinent and problems that human beings still face.

Name _____ Date _____

Final Test: *Romeo and Juliet*

Complete the following statements in the fewest possible words.

1. When we first meet Romeo in the play, he thinks he is in love with _____ .

2. The event that changes his mind is the _____ .

3. Romeo and Juliet are called "star-crossed lovers." Their love was doomed because their families

   _____ .

4. Several unlucky incidents illustrate that "the course of true love never did run smooth." One such
   incident involves Friar John, because he _____ .

5. Another is the meeting of Benvolio and Mercutio with Tybalt and Romeo's joining the first two a little
   later, because that meeting resulted in two deaths: _____'s and

   _____'s. It also resulted in Romeo's _____ .

6. Unintentionally, Balthasar gives a false report to Romeo, which eventually results in Romeo's

   _____ .

7. There are three peacemakers in the play; two of them are _____ and

   _____ .

8. The wittiest, most lighthearted character in the play is _____ .

9. A talkative and good-hearted, though somewhat unethical, female character in the play is

   _____ .

10. Capulet and Montague finally redeem themselves by _____ and by

    _____ .

11. The character in the play who is always angry and ready to pick a fight is _____ .

12. Juliet shows her courage when she accepts Friar Lawrence's desperate plan and decides to _____

    _____ .

13. Romeo's love for Juliet made him so gentle and peace-loving that he was reluctant to fight
    _____ and tried to send _____ away rather than fight him.

Who is the speaker in each of these quotations?

14. *But soft! What light through yonder window breaks?*   _____
    It is the East, and Juliet is the sun!

15. *'Tis but thy name that is my enemy.*   _____
    Thou art thyself, though not a Montague.

16. *Wisely and slow. They stumble that run fast.*   _____

17. *Well, sir, my mistress is the sweetest lady.*   _____
    Lord, Lord! when 'twas a little prating thing—

18. Which of the young people, Romeo or Juliet, do you think showed the greater maturity in the play?
    Explain. _____

19. Remember Lesson 8, "Examining the Themes in *Romeo and Juliet*." Which of the following do you
    consider the most important theme? Defend your choice on the back of this page.

    A. The course of true love never did run smooth.

    B. Violence brings about more violence.

    C. Moderation is the best policy.

    D. Disobedience to recognized authority inevitably brings retribution.

To the Teacher:

Suggestions for Presenting *Julius Caesar*

Sources for the Play

In Shakespeare's time, Roman history had great appeal for people of all ranks. The story of the rise and fall of Julius Caesar would have been generally known. Some might even have read the English translation of the Greek writer Plutarch's *Lives of Noble Grecians and Romans,* from which Shakespeare borrowed heavily to write *Julius Caesar.* Plutarch, who died in the second century A.D., produced a kind of biography of the lives of forty-six notable Greeks and Romans. They were arranged in groups of two—one Greek with one Roman—for purposes of comparison. His description of Caesar and the supernatural phenomena which occurred just before his death were used with very few changes in Shakespeare's play. Although Plutarch was writing about public figures, he showed these men in private moments as well, on the theory that when a public figure is "off stage," he is most apt to reveal his true character. It has been said that Shakespeare learned the art of depicting character and gained understanding of human beings in all their complexity from reading Plutarch.

During the sixteenth century, several Julius Caesar tragedies were performed on the continent and in England as well, but it remained for Shakespeare to produce the most memorable version of that great Roman's fall.

Topics for Class Discussion

Several volunteers could interview teachers (history or English) for their opinions of Caesar, who remains a controversial figure. The volunteers could then report their findings to the class. In a follow-up exercise, students could make a chalkboard list of Caesar's characteristics as revealed in the play. For example: Was he vain? cowardly? superstitious? Did he really want to become emperor, even though he refused the crown? As far as possible, students should support their opinions by citing incidents or speeches in the play.

Topics for Oral Reports

Ask some students to read a historical account of Caesar's life, including his relationship with Pompey. Have them recreate the facts as a story to tell in class.

Ask a few students to find the appropriate section in a translation of Plutarch's *Lives.* They may need a librarian's help on this. Ask them to see how closely Shakespeare followed Plutarch's account of the eve of Caesar's death, Caesar's assassination, and Portia's death. They can then report to the class.

Ask some students to find definitions of *mesomorph, endomorph*, and *ectomorph.* Ask them to look for additional information about the supposed relationship between body type and behavior. Caesar said of Cassius, "Yon Cassius has a lean and hungry look." What body type was he describing? Have the students report to the class, then ask their classmates to suggest prominent contemporary figures—sports heroes, movie stars, recent presidents, etc. In which of the three classifications does each fit?

Hands-On Activities

Cut out references to Shakespeare or his plays from newspapers and magazines for a bulletin-board display.

Students could make collages or sketches of their impressions of the characters for classroom display.

Ask the students to make a list of expressions in the play that they have heard before—for example, "Cowards die many times before their deaths." Students could then compare lists in class.

Vocabulary Building

In their notebooks, students should collect at least two unfamiliar words from each scene of the play, avoiding words that are footnoted. They should look up each word in a dictionary, define it, and write a sentence using it. In class, students can compare notes and learn from one another's work.

What Happens in Act I, *Julius Caesar*

Act I, Scene I On a street in Rome, two officials, Flavius and Marullus, meet a cobbler and a carpenter who have taken the day off to welcome home Caesar after his military triumph. Flavius and Marullus succeed in driving them from the street by calling them fickle. They remind them that not long before, they had turned out to welcome Pompey, who is now dead. (It is Pompey's sons whom Caesar has just defeated.)

Act I, Scene II Everyone has gathered to celebrate the Feast of Lupercal (February 15). Caesar stands with his wife, Calpurnia, and his friend Mark Antony. Suddenly, a fortune-teller calls out to Caesar from the crowd, warning him to "Beware the ides of March" (March 15). Meanwhile, two noble Romans, Cassius and Brutus, at a little distance apart from everyone else, are talking. When Brutus says that he won't stay for the festivities, Cassius seems hurt and says that Brutus is not as friendly to him as he used to be. Brutus apologizes, saying that if he neglects his friends, it is because his mind is troubled. Cassius uses that opportunity to find out how Brutus feels about Caesar and says that he fears the people will make Caesar king. Brutus says that he too has been concerned about that possibility. Then another friend, Casca, comes along. Casca says

that the people have offered Caesar the crown three times. but he has refused, each time more reluctantly, or so Casca thinks. Casca then leaves, and Brutus follows after promising to meet Cassius the next day. Alone on the stage, Cassius congratulates himself that he has already influenced Brutus. By trickery, he plans to win Brutus over to his way of thinking.

Act I, Scene III During a nighttime storm, Cicero, a senator, meets Casca, who talks wildly and fearfully about the storm and about strange things that have taken place that night. He believes that they are omens of things to come. Having said goodnight to Cicero, Casca goes on to meet Cassius. Cassius scolds Casca for his fears and compares the night to Caesar himself, who now strikes fear into the hearts of many Romans. Casca then suggests that the senators will make Caesar king. Cassius vows to kill himself rather than live in "bondage" (slavery) under Caesar. Having determined that Casca feels the same way, Cassius tells him that those who fear that Caesar is gaining too much power are meeting that very night. Cassius intends to make certain that Brutus joins them. He has thought of a trick to make Brutus believe that many citizens of Rome fear Caesar and admire Brutus.

The Ides of March

23   *The Complete Guide to Shakespeare's Best Plays*

Lesson 9: Understanding What You Have Read

> You know, of course, that the **plot** is the story—what happens and why. If you can answer the following questions on Act I, you have followed the plot so far.

1 In Scene I, Flavius and Marullus represent a higher class than that of the cobbler and the carpenter. How does their attitude toward Caesar contrast with the attitude of the two workingmen?

_____

2. In Scene I, you have an indication that Caesar is not popular with everyone in Rome. Scene II makes this point even clearer. The ordinary people love Caesar, but he has enemies among the more influential people. What is their objection to Caesar and to his being made king?

_____

3. In Scene III, what has only been hinted at becomes clear. A group of conspirators are determined to prevent Caesar from gaining more power.

   A. Who seems to be their leader? _____

   B. What one man are they eager to win over to their side? _____

   C. How does their leader propose to do this? _____

   _____

   D. Do you think it significant that they meet at night? Explain. _____

   _____

The second important element in a play is the **setting**—the time and place of the action. It influences how you, the reader or viewer, interpret the events. It also strengthens the plot. For example, in Scene III, the conspirators meet "under cover of darkness," making them seem evil and menacing to the reader. Now let's look more closely at the setting of Act I.

4. Scene I opens on a seemingly happy occasion, a holiday celebrating the triumphant return of Caesar to Rome. What mars the happiness of this scene?

   _____

5. Scene II is also a seemingly festive occasion; everyone is in the streets for the Lupercal.

   A. How does the warning called to Caesar by a man in the crowd change the festive mood?

   _____

   B. How does Brutus's, Cassius's, and Casca's conversation detract from the festivities?

   _____

   C. Does Caesar's attack of the "falling sickness" also alter the mood of the scene?

   _____

6. In Scene III, the gods are angry at humankind, or so the Romans would have believed. There is a terrible storm; a lion roams the streets of the city; people report having seen fire falling from the heavens and men all aflame walking the streets. The festive setting of Scenes I and II has changed to an ominous one that seems to indicate more evil to come. What do you expect may happen next?

   _____

Lesson 10: More Questions to Test Your Understanding of the Play So Far

To understand a play, you must be able to follow the action (the plot). The brief summaries of each act should help you. You must also be aware of the setting and understand how the playwright uses it to emphasize certain parts of the plot. Above all, you must get acquainted with the **characters**— with their physical appearance, of course, but also with their thoughts, their motivations or reasons for doing things, their weaknesses, and their strengths. As you read about what the characters do and say, as well as what others say about them, they should "come alive" for you.

1. While none of the characters in Scene I appears in the play again, Shakespeare makes them believable individuals.

   A. Is the cobbler truly respectful to his superior, Marullus? Explain.
   _____

   B. What evidence do you have that the cobbler has a good sense of humor and a way with words? (You may need to review his speeches to answer this question.)
   _____

2. In Scene II, you meet Caesar. Reread his comments to Antony about Cassius in the speech that begins, "Let me have men about me that are fat." (line 192)

   A. Does Caesar understand what kind of man Cassius is? Explain.
   _____

   B. Caesar says that men like Cassius are to be feared. Do you think Caesar himself fears Cassius? Explain.
   _____

   C. What do you learn about Caesar's health in this scene? (Part of your information comes from Cassius's comments, part from Caesar's own remarks, and part from what happens while Caesar is being offered the crown.)
   _____

3. In Scene II, you are introduced to Caesar's close friend, Mark Antony.

   A. What indications do you have that Mark Antony is quite young? (Remember Caesar's request to him as the scene opens.)
   _____

   B. How does Brutus contrast himself with Antony?
   _____

   C. How does Caesar contrast Antony and Cassius in his speech, revealing his distrust of Cassius?
   _____

4. In Scene III you learn more about both Cassius and Casca.

   A. Contrast Cassius's and Casca's reaction to the violent storm. Which man shows more courage?
   _____

   B. Cassius actually uses the storm to his own advantage. How does he use it to make Casca even more distrustful of Caesar? (See the speech that begins in line 57.)
   _____

   C. How does Cassius make absolutely certain that Casca will be his loyal follower?
   _____

   D. You have already seen that Caesar is a good judge of men, for his evaluation of Cassius was accurate. Do you think Cassius is also a good judge of character? Explain.
   _____

Reading Quiz: *Julius Caesar,* **Act I**

1. Having succeeded in driving away the cobbler and the carpenter, what further efforts do Flavius and Marcullus make to lessen the importance of Caesar's return?

   _____

   _____

2. Why does Caesar ask Mark Antony to touch Calpurnia with the leather thong he will carry in the race that is part of the celebration of the Lupercal?

   _____

   _____

3. What does Cassius say was the outcome when he and Caesar plunged into the River Tiber to swim to a certain point?

   _____

   _____

4. What does Cassius say happened to Caesar during a campaign in Spain?

   _____

   _____

5. What two physical infirmities of Caesar do we now know about?

   _____

   _____

6. What trick will Cassius use to make Brutus believe that many citizens of Rome respect Brutus and are fearful of Caesar's ambition?

   _____

   _____

7. If Caesar should be made king, how does Cassius intend to deliver himself from bondage?

   _____

   _____

8. Why are the conspirators so eager to make Brutus part of their group?

   _____

   _____

What Happens in Act II, *Julius Caesar*

Act II, Scene I Brutus, still troubled after his conversation about Julius Caesar with Cassius, has spent the night pacing up and down in his garden (orchard). Just before dawn, he rouses his young servant, Lucius, to bring a candle in his study. After the boy leaves, Brutus talks aloud to himself (soliloquy), allowing us to know what he is thinking. He is convinced that Caesar must die. Although he has no personal grudge against Caesar, Brutus fears that Caesar, once crowned king, will abuse his power. Lucius returns with a letter. (It is one that Cassius has directed a conspirator, or fellow plotter, to throw in through Brutus's window.) Brutus reads it and assumes that it is from the citizens of Rome who want him to act against Caesar.

While it is still dark, the conspirators arrive, led by Cassius. Brutus shakes hands with each one, pledging his support for their undertaking (the murder of Caesar), but he declines to swear an oath. Since they are men of honor, he believes that they don't need to make any promises. Cassius suggests that Mark Antony should be assassinated, too. Brutus disagrees because he believes that Antony, without Caesar, will be powerless. More important, he sees Caesar's killing as a sacrifice for the good of Rome, but he wants no further bloodshed.

Cassius fears that Caesar, being superstitious, may choose not to go to the Senate in the morning, since it is the ides of March. Decius claims that he can flatter Caesar into going. Before leaving, the conspirators agree to meet at 8:00 A.M. at Caesar's house. Brutus sends word to Caius Ligarius, who, he knows, will want to join them.

Portia, Brutus's wife, sees the conspirators leave. She comes in, knowing her husband is troubled, and begs him to tell her his secret. They are interrupted by a knock. Brutus asks her to leave, promising that later he will tell her the secrets of his heart. The new visitor is Caius Ligarius, who has been ill but is eager to follow Brutus's lead and become part of the conspiracy.

Act II, Scene II Early on the morning of the ides of March, Caesar is wakeful because of the previous night's terrible storm and his wife Calpurnia's troubled sleep. He tells a servant to have the priests prepare a sacrifice to see whether or not the omens for the day are favorable. Calpurnia comes in. Deeply disturbed by the strange storm and by her dreams, she begs Caesar not to go out that day because she fears for his life. Caesar's attitude is fatalistic. He says that whatever will be, will be. He tells her that cowards fear death but that he is not afraid. The servant comes back to report unfavorable omens. Calpurnia then pleads so urgently that Caesar agrees to stay home.

Decius arrives. Hearing that Caesar is not planning to go to the Senate, Decius cleverly manipulates him by reinterpreting Calpurnia's dream to make it sound favorable to Caesar. He says that the senators intend to offer him a crown that day, but if they learn that Caesar will not go out because of his wife's worrisome dream, they may change their minds.

Won over by these arguments, Caesar agrees to go to the Senate. The other conspirators arrive to accompany him. Caesar offers them wine before they leave his house, a kind gesture that makes Brutus feel guilty.

Act II, Scene III Artemidorus, who admires Caesar, waits along the way to the Senate, intending to pass Caesar a letter warning of the conspiracy.

Act II, Scene IV Portia, fearful of what she suspects is to take place that day, sends Lucius to the Senate House. Because she cannot let the boy know her fears, she tells him only to see whether or not his master looks well and to tell Brutus that she is cheerful. She then speaks to a soothsayer, or fortune-teller, who intends to warn Caesar.

Name _____   Date _____

Lesson 11:
Getting Acquainted with the Characters in *Julius Caesar*

The first lesson dealing with *Julius Caesar* was aimed at helping you understand the plot and setting of the play. The second lesson emphasized certain qualities of three important characters—Caesar, Cassius, and Mark Antony. Act II focuses on the fourth major character, Brutus, but it also acquaints you with the two wives, Calpurnia and Portia, and reveals new details of Caesar's character.

After reading the summary of Act II and then reading Act II itself, you should be able to answer the following questions.

1. In Act II, Scene I, Brutus envies his soundly sleeping young servant. Portia, Brutus's wife, comments later in this scene that Brutus got up in the night, left the bedroom, and did not return. What is the apparent cause of Brutus's restlessness and inability to sleep?

   _____

2. Since Brutus has no personal grudge against Caesar, of what must he convince himself before he can take part in Caesar's assassination?

   _____

3. At this point, what adjectives would you use to describe Brutus's character?

   _____

4. Cassius, unlike Brutus, is partly motivated by personal dislike of Caesar. What do you think is the underlying cause of this dislike?

   _____

5. From the comments of Cassius and Brutus (lines 154–191), what conflicting views of the character of Mark Antony do you get?

   _____

6. A. By what means does Decius promise to bring Caesar to the Senate House?

   _____

   B. What does his promised course of action show you about his character?

   _____

7. What qualities of Portia do you find especially admirable?

   _____

8. What qualities, if any, do Portia and Calpurnia have in common?

   _____

9. How does Calpurnia's relationship with Caesar seem to differ from Portia's relationship with Brutus?

   _____

10. What indications do you have in Act II that Caesar is:

    A. superstitious _____

    B. proud _____

    C. a courageous soldier _____

    D. influenced by flattery _____

    E. considerate, trusting, and generous to his friends _____

    _____

             The Complete Guide to Shakespeare's Best Plays

Reading Quiz: *Julius Caesar,* **Act II**

1. Brutus states in his soliloquy that up to now, Caesar has not let his emotions sway his judgment as a ruler. Why, then, does Brutus fear for the future if Caesar is crowned king?

   _____

   _____

2. Since Cassius first mentioned to Brutus his fears about Caesar's ambition, what does Brutus say his frame of mind has been?

   _____

   _____

3. Why does Brutus object to having Cicero as one of the conspirators?

   _____

   _____

4. What is Brutus's opinion of Mark Antony?

   _____

   _____

5. Before asking her husband to tell her his secrets, what physical act does Portia perform to prove her strength of character?

   _____

   _____

6. What has made Portia suspicious of the men who visited Brutus in his garden?

   _____

   _____

7. Who arrives at Caesar's house just after the conspirators but is not one of them?

   _____

   _____

What Happens in Act III, *Julius Caesar*

Act III, Scene I At the Capitol, the soothsayer again tries to warn Caesar, who does not listen. Nor is Artemidorus successful. Caesar refuses to read his letter, but the conspirators realize that their plot is known. They find an excuse to get Mark Antony out of the Capitol. Then Metellus Cimber approaches Caesar with a request that he knows Caesar will not grant. (He's asking pardon for a brother who has been banished.) Brutus and Cassius now add their pleas to Metellus's as the other conspirators move close to Caesar. Caesar tells them all that "like the northern star," he cannot be swayed from his true course. Publius Cimber deserved his banishment; Caesar will not recall him.

All at once, the conspirators stab Caesar. Brutus strikes the last blow; when Caesar realizes that his friend Brutus is part of the conspiracy, he collapses and dies. The assassins now realize that they must explain their deed to the people and convince them that they acted to destroy tyranny. Brutus insists that each conspirator bathe his hands in Caesar's blood to show the Romans that this was a sacrificial killing.

Mark Antony's servant comes to ask Brutus if it is safe for his master to come to the Capitol. He wants to learn from Brutus why Caesar had to die. Brutus says that he may come, and Caesar's killing will be explained to him. Antony arrives and first addresses Caesar's corpse, "O mighty Caesar! Dost thou lie so low?" Then he turns to the conspirators, saying that if he is among those yet to be killed, let them kill him now. Brutus assures him that they have done what they had to do for the citizens of Rome. He tells Antony that they want to make him one of them, and Cassius promises him a post in the new government. Antony shakes hands with the conspirators, but turns to speak again to Caesar's corpse, asking pardon for making peace with his assassins. Cassius, ever suspicious, asks Antony if they can count him a friend. He says yes, but he must know why Caesar was slain. Brutus assures him that his question will be answered.

Antony asks permission to take Caesar's body to the marketplace and deliver the funeral speech.

Brutus agrees, despite Cassius's objections. Brutus says that he himself will speak first, then Antony. Antony must state that he is speaking with Brutus's permission. He may praise Caesar but may not blame the conspirators. Antony agrees.

After the conspirators' departure, Antony's soliloquy shows his anger and his determination that Caesar's death be avenged. He predicts civil war, death, and destruction. Octavius, Caesar's servant, arrives to tell him that Octavius (Julius's grandnephew) is close to Rome. Antony tells him that Rome is not safe for his master as yet, but that Antony will know the mood of the people better after the funeral speech.

Act III, Scene II In the marketplace, Brutus addresses the citizens of Rome, explaining that though he loved and honored Caesar, he loved Rome more. He killed Caesar because Caesar was too ambitious and would have enslaved his countrymen. He concludes that as he used his dagger on Caesar for Rome's sake, he would use it on himself for Rome's sake if necessary. The citizens greet his speech with shouts of approval. Brutus leaves after telling the people to stay to listen to Mark Antony. Antony begins by saying that Brutus and his friends, all honorable men, have said that because Caesar was too ambitious, he had to die. He then reminds them that Caesar, the general, brought many captives to Rome and that their ransoms went into the general treasury, not into Caesar's pocket. He reminds them that Caesar refused the crown three times and tells them that Caesar loved and wept for the poor. He asks them if these were the deeds of an ambitious man. He reminds them how much they once loved Caesar, yet are not mourning him now. He shows them Caesar's body, mutilated by stab wounds, and tells them that they, the ordinary people, are the beneficiaries of Caesar's will. Now wildly angry against the conspirators, the citizens rush off, bent on destruction.

Act III, Scene III In this brief scene, the angry mob kills an innocent man (Cinna the poet), a friend of Caesar, simply because he has the same name as one of the conspirators.

Lesson 12:
Understanding the Characters' Behavior

At the beginning of Act III, Shakespeare gives us two more glimpses of Caesar's character. Questions 1 and 2 test your understanding of Caesar's **motivations** (reasons for doing things). Answering these questions may help you decide whether or not Caesar was the kind of person the conspirators believed him to be.

1. A. When Artemidorus first urges Caesar to read his letter, why does Caesar refuse?

   _____

   B. Artemidorus insists that Caesar read the letter. What is Caesar's reaction?

   _____

   C. What two characteristics of Caesar's do your answers to A and B reveal?

   _____

2. Review Caesar's two speeches, the first, beginning "I must prevent thee, Cimber," lines 35–48, and the second, beginning "I could be well moved, if I were as you," lines 58–73.
   A. Based on the first speech, what seems to be Caesar's reaction to flattery?

   _____

   B. In the second speech, what does Caesar say his course of action is, once he has made a decision?

   _____

   C. Are the qualities Caesar reveals in the two speeches desirable in a ruler? Explain.

   _____

3. Why is it so important to Brutus that the conspirators bathe their hands in Caesar's blood?

   _____

4. Why do you think Mark Antony sends a message to Brutus, not Cassius, asking safe conduct if he returns to the Capitol?

   _____

5. After shaking hands with the conspirators, Antony turns again to Caesar's corpse and asks forgiveness.
   A. At this point, do you think Antony is moved solely by grief, or do you think he is doing what he believes the conspirators would expect him to do? Give a reason for your choice.

   _____

   B. Whatever his motives, would Antony's behavior make the conspirators more or less trustful of him? Explain.

   _____

6. Basing your answer on what happens later in this act, state who was the better judge of Antony and his power over the people: Brutus or Cassius. Explain your choice.

   _____

7. Look now at Brutus's and Antony's speeches to the citizens of Rome. Brutus's speech is brief. He tells the citizens what we, the readers, already know—that though Caesar was his friend, he killed him for the good of Rome. He says he would be willing to kill himself for Rome's sake if the sacrifice were required. Is Brutus sincere? Refer specifically to his actions up to this point. _____

8. Antony's speech has a much greater emotional appeal than Brutus's, and it is very clever argumentation.
   A. How does he disprove Brutus's claim that Caesar was too ambitious?

   _____

   B. What dramatic act of Antony's stirs the people to frenzy? _____
   C. Why does he withhold Caesar's will until late in his speech?

   _____

Reading Quiz: *Julius Caesar,* **Act III**

1. After Cassius offers Antony a place in the new government and they shake hands, what does Antony do that causes Cassius to doubt that he is truly a friend to the conspirators?

_____

_____

2. What is Antony's true opinion of the conspirators? (He tells us in his soliloquy.)

_____

_____

3. Why has Octavius Caesar come to Rome?

_____

_____

4. What are the terms of Caesar's will?

_____

_____

5. Whom does Antony join after his speech in the marketplace?

_____

_____

6. By the end of the scene in the marketplace, what has become of Brutus and Cassius?

_____

_____

7. In Scene III, in which Cinna the poet meets some citizens of Rome, what lesson is Shakespeare teaching us about the character of a mob?

_____

_____

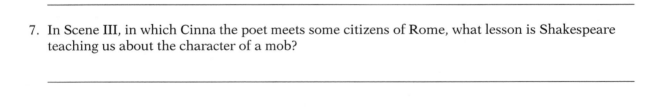

What Happens in Act IV, *Julius Caesar*

Act IV, Scene I Antony, Octavius Caesar, and Lepidus now rule Rome. In Antony's house, they are preparing a list of people (including Lepidus's brother and Antony's nephew) to execute or banish.

Antony, who intends to eliminate some of the bequests in Caesar's will, sends Lepidus to get it and bring it to them. As soon as Lepidus leaves, Antony belittles him to Octavius and says they should not make him their equal in power. Octavius defends Lepidus, saying he is a good soldier, but then tells Antony to do as he pleases.

The two discuss their uncertain position, surrounded by people they do not trust and threatened by Brutus and Cassius, who are raising an army and will challenge them.

Act IV, Scene II Cassius's servant, Pindarus, has just brought his master's greeting to Brutus, whose army is encamped near Sardis. Brutus's friend Lucilius, who has just returned from Cassius's camp, says that Cassius seemed only polite, not friendly.

When Cassius arrives with his officers, he immediately accuses Brutus of wronging him. Brutus refuses to discuss their differences until they are alone.

Act IV, Scene III In Brutus's tent, he and Cassius quarrel. Cassius is angry because Brutus condemned Lucius Pella for bribery despite Cassius's letters in Pella's behalf. Brutus replies that Cassius should not have defended such a man and insults Cassius further, accusing him of greediness and graft. Brutus tells Cassius that he, one of the men who killed Caesar "for justice's sake," should not now stoop to bribery and graft. Cassius says he is holding back his temper only because it is Brutus who accuses him; another man would die for such insults. Brutus continues to taunt him. He accuses Cassius of failing him when he asked for money to pay his troops.

Cassius denies that he refused Brutus's request. Then he breaks down, saying that Brutus, his friend, has turned against him and now recites all his faults. He offers Brutus his dagger and his

life. Brutus, apparently moved, says that he spoke out of ill temper. Cassius apologizes for his own anger, and the quarrel is over.

Only then does Brutus tell Cassius of his great grief; Portia has committed suicide. Cassius is overwhelmed by the sad news, but Brutus, the Stoic, says they will speak no more of his loss and bids the servant bring them a bowl of wine. They then plan their strategy with the other officers since Antony and Octavius, with their armies, are marching to Philippi. Cassius favors remaining at Sardis. Antony and Octavius would have to march to meet them and would arrive with their troops tired and at a disadvantage. Brutus prefers to move to Philippi and confront the enemies. Brutus's will prevails.

The others leave, and Brutus then asks his servant, Lucius, to tell Varro and Claudius that they may sleep in Brutus's tent. Lucius falls asleep while playing his lute to soothe Brutus. Brutus, still sleepless, begins to read. Caesar's ghost enters, tells Brutus they will meet again at Philippi, and disappears. Brutus wakes the others. He asks them why they cried out in their sleep and if they saw anything. They, of course, did not. He then sends word to Cassius that they must get their armies underway.

Lesson 13: What is Significant in Act IV?

1. A. How does Antony reveal himself as both cold-blooded and cruel in Scene I of this act?

    _____

    B. Did his behavior in the previous act prepare you for this side of Antony's character? Use examples to support your answer.

    _____

    _____

2. Until this act, Cassius has seemed totally cold and calculating. In his final reaction to Brutus's accusations and his reaction to the news of Portia's death, what new details of his character are revealed?

    _____

3. Where in this act does Brutus show each of the following?
    A. stern self-control _____
    B. tenderness _____
    C. contempt _____
    D. self-righteousness _____

4. Brutus accuses Cassius of graft, yet he himself had asked Cassius for money to pay his troops. Brutus would not stoop to obtaining money by "vile means" (that is, through dishonest practices). However, he would have been willing to use the money Cassius obtained that way. What weakness of character does Brutus display here?

    _____

5. Shakespeare believed that if a rightful ruler was deposed or assassinated, only disaster could follow—not only for those involved in overthrowing the ruler, but also for the country itself.
    A. So far, what events in Rome support Shakespeare's belief?

    _____

    B. What event is about to happen in the next act that would give further support to this belief?

    _____

6. Brutus believed that Caesar was too ambitious and might have become a danger to Rome. What other people in the play seem to be motivated by too much ambition or hunger for power? What have been the results of this ambition?

    _____

    _____

7. In Scene III, Brutus, justifying his belief that he and Cassius should move their armies to Philippi to meet the enemies, says:

    > *There is a tide in the affairs of men*   *not taken advantage of
    > *Which, taken at the flood, leads on to fortune;* **everything we have at stake
    > *Omitted,* all the voyage of their life*
    > *Is bound in shallows and in miseries.*
    > *On such a full sea are we now afloat,*
    > *And we must take the current when it serves*
    > *Or lose our ventures.***

    First, restate Brutus's speech in your own words. Use the back of this sheet to write your answer. Then explain why you agree or disagree with Brutus's idea.

Reading Quiz: *Julius Caesar,* **Act IV**

1. By what means did Portia commit suicide?

   _____

2. According to letters that Brutus and Messala have received, approximately how many people have Antony, Octavius, and Lepidus already put to death in Rome?

   _____

3. What does Brutus fear will happen along the way if Antony's and Octavius's armies march from Philippi to Sardis?

   _____

   _____

4. What message does Caesar's ghost have for Brutus?

   _____

   _____

5. Brutus and Cassius disagree about whether or not their armies should march to Philippi, and Cassius concedes to Brutus. On what two occasions earlier in the play have they disagreed about which course to follow? (On these two occasions also it was Brutus's judgment that prevailed.)

   _____

   _____

What Happens in Act V, *Julius Caesar*

Act V, Scene I As Brutus's and Cassius's armies approach Philippi, Octavius and Antony discuss battle strategy. Antony tries to take supreme command, but Octavius calmly opposes him.

Before the battle begins, the four opposing commanders have a discussion, but much of their talk is simply an exchange of insults. Finally, Octavius, impatient with the delay, says that he will avenge Caesar's death or die in the attempt. Then he calls Antony away after challenging Brutus and Cassius to battle when they "dare fight."

Cassius talks with his friend Messala. It is Cassius's birthday, but his spirits are low. On the march to Philippi, he observed certain bad omens and now he expects defeat in the upcoming battle.

When Cassius asks Brutus what he will do if they lose the battle, Brutus says that he considers suicide "cowardly," yet he would never return to Rome as a captive. The two friends then bid each other farewell, accepting the strong possibility that they will never meet again.

Act V, Scene II Brutus, judging that Octavius's troops lack fighting spirit, sends Messala with a message to Cassius to make a surprise attack.

Act V, Scene III The battle is going badly for Cassius. He was not able to prevent his men's retreat from Antony's troops. His servant Pindarus now begs him to flee. From the vantage point of a hill, Cassius can see his tents on fire and soldiers milling about, but he doesn't know if they are friends or enemies. He sends Titinius to bring him a report, and then asks Pindarus to go higher on the hill and observe Titinius as he rides toward the camp. Pindarus reports that Titinius has been surrounded and taken by the enemy. Cassius can bear no more. He gives Pindarus his sword (the sword he used to kill Caesar) and tells Pindarus to kill him. Pindarus obeys, Cassius dies, and Pindarus flees. Titinius returns with Messala, who has good news that Brutus has defeated Octavius. They find Cassius dead. Messala goes to carry the sad news to Brutus. Titinius, knowing that Cassius must have died

because he assumed they were defeated, kills himself.

Brutus, Messala, and the other officers arrive and find the corpses. Brutus sees their deaths as part of Caesar's revenge. Though Brutus is grieved by Cassius's death, he orders his funeral to be held at a distant place so that the troops' morale will not suffer, and he plans a second battle.

Act V, Scene IV In battle, Lucilius pretends to be Brutus, hoping he will be killed in Brutus's place. The enemy soldiers, reluctant to kill the noble Brutus, take him prisoner instead. When Antony sees him, he tells the soldiers to treat Lucillus kindly but to continue to hunt for Brutus, dead or alive.

Act V, Scene V Meanwhile, Brutus, knowing they are defeated, asks each of his friends, in turn, to kill him. Clitus, Dardanius, and Volumnius refuse; as the enemies approach, Brutus then asks them to flee. Finally, Brutus persuades his servant Strato to hold the sword while he runs into it, killing himself.

Octavius and Antony arrive with Messala and Lucilius, now prisoners. Strato reports how Brutus died. Antony gives the final tribute, "This was the noblest Roman of them all." Octavius orders that Brutus be given all the respect and rites due a soldier of his rank. Octavius has the final word: "Let's away, To part the glories [divide the honors] of this happy day."

Lesson 14: Examining the Themes in *Julius Caesar*

In an earlier lesson, you learned that the theme of a piece of literature is its central idea, which can be stated in general terms. *Julius Caesar* has several themes, some more important than others. They might be listed like this:

A. An idealistic person (Brutus) can be manipulated by a clever and perhaps dishonest person (Cassius).

B. If the rightful ruler is deposed or killed, chaos will result.

C. Ordinary people (the crowd) are easily swayed by effective speech-making; thus, they can be changed into a dangerous mob. Shakespeare shows us that the crowd is fickle.

D. Ambitions can change a man's character so that he no longer seeks good for all men but rather seeks more power for himself.

E. Power tends to corrupt those who hold it.

F. People can easily convince themselves that the end justifies any means.

1. State when in the play theme A is developed; that is, when is Brutus manipulated by Cassius?

_____

Why, later on, does Cassius let his judgment be swayed by Brutus?

_____

_____

2. Theme B can, of course, be applied to Caesar's assassination and what follows. You have already considered this theme in *Julius Caesar* in an earlier lesson. Now show briefly how chaos developed after Caesar's death.

_____

_____

3. Theme C is easily demonstrated. Who turned the crowd into a mob? How did he do it? What actions did the mob take?

_____

_____

4. Theme D might have applied to Caesar's future actions. Brutus believed it would. Could you apply theme D to any other character in the play? Explain.

_____

_____

5. What is the best illustration of theme E in the play? _____

_____

6. Can you apply theme F to Brutus's actions? To Cassius's actions? Explain.

_____

_____

Reading Quiz: *Julius Caesar,* **Act V**

1. What bad omens did Cassius see during the march to Philippi?

   _____

2. What was actually happening to Titinius when Pindarus incorrectly reported that he was being taken by the enemy?

   _____

3. After Pindarus slays Cassius (as Cassius had requested), what happens to Pindarus?

   _____

4. Remember that Caesar died on the ides of March (the 15th). What is significant about the day of Cassius's death?

   _____

5. How does Titinius show his grief at Cassius's death?

   _____

6. Whose visits to Brutus, both at Sardis and Philippi, have made Brutus certain that the hour of his death is near?

   _____

7. Antony called Brutus "the noblest Roman of them all" because _____

   _____ .

Name _____ Date _____

Final Test: *Julius Caesar*

Complete the following statements in the fewest possible words.

1. Brutus's reason for entering the conspiracy was _____ .

2. Cassius's motive for killing Caesar was _____ .

3. The night before Caesar's death was remarkable because of such strange occurrences as

    _____

4. Brutus urged the other conspirators to bathe their hands in Caesar's blood because he wanted to believe

    that they had committed a _____ , not a _____ .

5. Misjudging Antony's character, Brutus allowed him to _____ .

6. The fate of Cinna the poet demonstrates that _____ .

7. Caesar revealed that he could be influenced by flattery when he allowed Decius Brutus to _____

    _____

8. When Caesar said, "Cowards die many times before their deaths; The valiant never taste of death but

    once," he showed his _____ . (a characteristic)

9. Cassius reveals his genuine affection for Brutus when, after their argument, Brutus tells him the sad

    news about _____ .

A **symbol** represents something besides the thing it actually names. For example, the term *red rose* names a
beautiful flower, but a red rose can represent or symbolize sexual love or passion. Each of the following in
Julius Caesar names an actual condition, but it is also a symbol of something more.

10. Caesar's "falling sickness" or epilepsy symbolizes _____ .
    Clue: What happens to Caesar's power and his life?

11. Caesar's deafness symbolizes _____ .
    Clue: Remember the soothsayer, Artemidorus, and Caesar's priests.

12. Brutus's sleeplessness symbolizes _____ .
    Clue: Remember that Brutus envies Lucius, who sleeps the innocent sleep of a child.

Which of the major characters is described in each of the following quotations?

13. Caesar's comment: *Yon _____ has a lean and hungry look.*
    He thinks too much. Such men are dangerous.   Caesar refers to _____ .

14. Antony's comment: *This was the noblest Roman of them all.*   *except
    All the conspirators save* only he
    Did that they did in envy of great Caesar.   Antony refers to _____ .

15. Antony's comment: *When that the poor have cried, _____ hath wept.*
    Ambition should be made of sterner stuff.   Antony refers to _____ .

Who is the speaker of these quotations? (Imagine what situation would make the speech appropriate.)

16.   *Men at some time are masters of their fates:*   *subordinate
    The fault, dear Brutus, is not in our stars,
    But in ourselves, that we are underlings*.   The speaker is _____ .

17.   *Our course shall seem too bloody, Caius Cassius,*
    To cut the head off and then hack the limbs.   The speaker is _____ .

18. Based on your understanding of the play, what is your opinion of Caesar? Refer to the play to support
    that opinion. Write your answer on the back of this page.

To the Teacher:

Suggestions for Presenting *Macbeth*

Source

In finding background information for one of his truly great plays, *Macbeth*, Shakespeare depended on a contemporary historian, Raphael Holinshed. Holinshed's *Chronicles of England, Scotland and Ireland* was first published in 1577, with a second edition appearing in 1587. Scholars believe Shakespeare relied heavily on the 1587 edition for his so-called English-history plays. As in his use of Plutarch's *Lives* for his Roman-history plays, Shakespeare adopted many lines from Holinshed with little or no change.

Politically speaking, Shakespeare was a royalist (believer in the monarchy). What is more, he and his company of actors depended upon their royal patron King James I's generosity. In telling the Macbeth story, Shakespeare was showing his audience that when a rightful monarch (Duncan) is murdered, chaos follows. Since James I was on the English throne at the time and, as a descendant of Banquo, was the rightful monarch, that message must have pleased the king greatly.

Topics for Class Discussion

Ask several students to read an account of the Salem witch trials that took place in seventeenth-century New England, the same century in which *Macbeth* was written. The students should then report to the class, emphasizing that in both the old and new world of the seventeenth century, belief in witches was common. Students can discuss whether they think people today are as superstitious as people of that earlier time. They will need examples to support their points of view.

Other students might like to read *The Crucible*, a modern retelling of the events of the Salem

witch trials. Some of the students might write reviews of *The Crucible* to read in class. Students should then be asked to prove or disprove that we are still susceptible to superstitious hysteria.

Topics for Oral Reports

Ask two students to check an encyclopedia or other reference and find out as much as possible about either James I or Edward the Confessor and report to the class.

Ask other students to find pictures of Scottish castles still in existence. *National Geographic* would be a good source. Then have students read about castle life in the eleventh century (the time of Macbeth) and report to the class, using the pictures of castles to illustrate.

In a history of the theater or similar reference, students can find pictures of Macbeth and Lady Macbeth as they have been portrayed on the stage. The pictures and the information about actors who have played these roles can be used as the basis of a class report.

Hands-On Activities

Ask one or more students to make a poster for the bulletin board depicting the three witches in *Macbeth*. All of the details Shakespeare gives about the witches should be included.

Vocabulary Building

In their notebooks, students should collect at least two unfamiliar words from each scene of the play, avoiding words that are footnoted. They should look up each word in a dictionary, define it, and write a sentence using it. In class, students can compare notes and learn from one another's work.

What Happens in Act I, *Macbeth*

Act I, Scene I During a thunderstorm, three witches discuss when they will meet again. It is to be that very day, after a battle, on a heath (an open space with little vegetation) where they will meet Macbeth.

Act I, Scene II At a battle camp, King Duncan, his sons Malcolm and Donalbain, Lennox, and others talk to a sergeant, who reports on the battle. Macdonwald, a rebel with an army, has been vanquished and killed by one of Duncan's generals, Macbeth. Then the Norwegian king, hoping that Duncan's forces are at a disadvantage, has attacked, but when the sergeant leaves, Macbeth and Banquo are holding their own against him. Ross comes in to report that the Thane of Cawdor has turned traitor and joined the Norwegian forces, but Macbeth has now defeated them. Ross says the Norwegian king begs for a peace treaty and will pay tribute. Pleased at this news, Duncan pronounces a death sentence on Cawdor and says that his title will go to Macbeth.

Act I, Scene III On a heath, the witches meet again, each reporting on the mischief she has been making. Macbeth and Banquo happen upon them, and Banquo speaks first, although he is uncertain whether they are women or spirits. The witches greet Macbeth, first by his actual title, then as Thane of Cawdor, and finally as he who shall be king. Macbeth seems startled by their greeting. Banquo speaks to them again, asking what they can predict for him. Meanwhile, Macbeth recovers himself and asks them to explain their prediction, but they vanish. As Banquo and Macbeth discuss this strange experience, Ross and Angus arrive to tell Macbeth that Duncan has made him Thane of Cawdor. Macbeth is struck by the accuracy of the witches' prophecy and asks Banquo if he thinks their prediction for him will come true. Banquo fears the witches may be instruments of the devil, but Macbeth's imagination is stirred, and the thoughts that come into his mind horrify him. To Banquo he says only that they must talk further of the day's events.

Act I, Scene IV At the palace, Malcolm reports to his father that Cawdor is dead. Macbeth, Banquo, and the others arrive. Duncan greets Macbeth

warmly. He then announces that Malcolm is to be his successor to the throne. Macbeth, troubled at this turn of events, leaves to inform his wife that the king will visit them at Inverness.

Act I, Scene V At their castle, Lady Macbeth has had a letter from Macbeth, telling her of the witches' prophecy. She knows that her husband is "too full o' the milk of human kindness" but intends to give him the determination to do what has to be done (murder Duncan) if he is to be king. Macbeth arrives, saying Duncan will be with them that very night. She begins to reveal her plan, but Macbeth is hesitant.

Act I, Scene VI Duncan arrives at the castle and is greeted by Lady Macbeth. She assures him that she is pleased to offer him hospitality, for she and her husband are ever in his debt.

Act I, Scene VII The dinner is almost over. Macbeth, alone for a moment, reveals his thoughts in a soliloquy (speech spoken when an actor is alone on the stage). He admits that it is only ambition that makes him consider killing a good man. When Lady Macbeth comes in, Macbeth says that he will not commit the murder. She calls him a coward and urges him so cleverly that he changes his mind once more. She then reveals her plan, dismissing Macbeth's objections.

Statue of Lady Macbeth, at Stratford-on-Avon

Name _____ Date _____

Lesson 15: Macbeth, A Tragic Figure

> *Macbeth*—like *Othello*, *Hamlet*, and *King Lear*—is one of Shakespeare's four great tragedies. Macbeth himself, like the **protagonists** (main characters) of the other three dramas, is a man capable of arousing our interest, even our sympathy, but he is a man with a **character flaw**. It is this fatal flaw that brings about his downfall.
>
> Before Macbeth ever appears on the stage, Shakespeare begins portraying his character. Our first knowledge of him comes from other characters' comments.

1. What evidence do we have in Act I, Scene II, of Macbeth's bravery?
   _____

2. What evidence is there that King Duncan respects Macbeth?
   _____

3. In Scene III, who seems more affected by the witches' prophecies, Macbeth or Banquo? Explain.
   _____

4. What indications are there in this scene that Macbeth is highly imaginative? (See especially lines 128–143.) _____

5. Is there any indication that the idea of killing Duncan has already occurred to him?
   _____

Note too in this scene Macbeth's asides (speeches not intended for the other characters' ears).

6. In Scene IV, what does Macbeth say is the duty of loyal subjects like himself to King Duncan? Is he sincere? _____

7. What happens in this scene that makes Macbeth vow that the evil deed he has been considering must be done? _____

8. What is Macbeth's tragic flaw? _____

9. In his conversation with Banquo in Scene II, Macbeth pretends to be somewhat disinterested in the witches' prophecies. What in Scene V proves that he has taken them very seriously?
   _____

10. From Lady Macbeth's soliloquy at the beginning of Scene V, what further insights into Macbeth's character do we gain?
    _____

11. Do you have the impression that Lady Macbeth and Macbeth have a loving relationship? Explain.
    _____

12. Who seems the stronger in Scene V, Lady Macbeth or Macbeth? Explain. _____
    _____

13. Reread Macbeth's famous soliloquy that opens Scene VII. What indication is there that Macbeth fears for the future if he should murder Duncan?
    _____

14. Does Macbeth see his own shortcomings clearly? Explain. _____
    _____

15. When Lady Macbeth accuses Macbeth of cowardice, he replies,
    > *Prithee [I pray you] peace:*
    > *I dare do all that may become a man.*
    > *Who dares do more is none.*

    What is your understanding of this speech? Is Macbeth accurately describing his life to this point?
    _____

Reading Quiz: *Macbeth,* Act I

1. How does the first witch plan to punish the sailor's wife who refused to give her chestnuts?

   _____

   _____

2. What do the witches predict for Banquo's future?

   _____

   _____

3. Aside from promising that Malcolm will be the next king, what title does Duncan give him?

   _____

   _____

4. On whom does Lady Macbeth call to give her the strength of purpose to perform Duncan's murder?

   _____

   _____

5. Macbeth gives three reasons why he should not kill Duncan. Name two of them.

   _____

   _____

6. What is Lady Macbeth's plan for killing the king?

   _____

   _____

What Happens in Act II, *Macbeth*

Act II, Scene I It is after midnight as Banquo comes in with his young son, Fleance. Banquo is reluctant to go to bed because he fears his sleep will be troubled. Macbeth comes in, and Banquo tells him that the king has gone to bed, having enjoyed the evening. Banquo then says he dreamed the previous night of the witches. Macbeth claims he gives no thought to them, but he suggests that they talk further about the witches at another time. He implies that if Banquo cooperates with him, he will be rewarded. Banquo replies that if he can gain the reward (honor) without behaving in a dishonorable or disloyal way, he will. He and Fleance leave. Macbeth sends a servant to Lady Macbeth asking her to summon him with a bell when his "drink is ready." Alone, he hallucinates, thinking he sees a dagger in the air. Just then, the bell summons him to the evil deed.

Act II, Scene II Lady Macbeth, alone, talks to herself about what she has done. She gave the king's grooms enough wine to make them drunk and drugged them besides. She put out their daggers for Macbeth and would have killed the king herself had he not reminded her of her father. Macbeth comes in to tell her the deed is done. He is unnerved because when the unsuspecting grooms prayed, he could not say, "Amen." She tells him not to dwell upon the deed but to get water and wash the blood from his hands. In his agitation, Macbeth has brought the grooms' daggers out of the room. She tells him to take them back and smear the sleeping grooms with blood, but he refuses. She then replaces the daggers herself. While he is alone, Macbeth hears knocking. Lady Macbeth returns; she too has heard the knocking. She says they must retire to their bedroom and put on nightclothes so that the visitors will think they have been asleep. Macbeth is regretting his deed and wishing Duncan were still alive.

Act II, Scene III The porter goes grumbling to open the gate as if he were opening the gates of Hell. (His soliloquy is intended as comic relief after the great tension of the previous scene.) The

visitors are Macduff and Lennox. When Macbeth appears, Macduff explains that he has an appointment with Duncan, and Macbeth takes him to the king's door. Macduff returns, horrified at the sight of his king, cruelly murdered. Macbeth and Lennox rush to Duncan's room while Macduff rouses the household. Macduff cannot bring himself to tell Lady Macbeth what has happened. When Banquo appears, Macduff tells him. Macbeth returns to make a grieving speech as Malcolm and Donalbain finally appear. When Malcolm asks who has killed his father, Lennox says that the grooms are apparently the villains. Macbeth "repents" that in his anger, he has killed the grooms on sight. Macduff questions why Macbeth killed them, and at that moment, Lady Macbeth faints. In the confusion that follows, Malcolm and Donalbain decide to flee since they think their father's murderer may strike them next. Meanwhile, at Banquo's suggestion, the others decide to meet to discuss what will happen.

Act II, Scene IV Ross and an old man discuss strange events that have immediately followed Duncan's death. Macduff appears, and Ross questions him about the king's murder: Macduff says it is believed that the grooms were the murderers, acting for someone else. Since the king's sons have fled, suspicion falls on them. Macduff also reports that Macbeth is to be the new king and that Duncan's body has been taken to the burial place of his ancestors. Macduff will not attend Macbeth's coronation; rather, he is returning home to Fife.

Lesson 16: Understanding Lady Macbeth

Shakespeare created a number of memorable female characters. Most were good women, such as Portia in *The Merchant of Venice* and Cordelia in *King Lear*. But also in *King Lear* were Cordelia's evil, grasping sisters, Goneril and Regan. No female character in Shakespeare's plays makes a more lasting impression than Lady Macbeth, however. For Shakespearean actresses, interpreting her character has become the ultimate test and triumph.

At this stage in the play, you cannot know or understand Lady Macbeth completely, but it is worthwhile to consider what her speeches and actions have already revealed.

1. From her first appearance in Act I, Scene V, it is obvious that Lady Macbeth is determined to commit murder if necessary to make Macbeth king. But why is she willing? Is it for the status and power that she will gain as queen, or is it simply because that is what Macbeth wants? The answer, in part, is in the letter from Macbeth to her and in her comments on it, in Scene V, lines 1–31. Reread the lines and state what you think her reason is.

   _____

2. Look closely now at these lines in the same speech:
   > What thou* wouldst** highly,   *you
   > That wouldst thou holily; wouldst not play false,   **would
   > And yet wouldst wrongly win.

   Note that *would* is still used in expressing a wish or desire, as in *I would I were young again.*
   What is she saying about her husband's wishes and character?

   _____

3. In what sense does Lady Macbeth think she must be strong for her husband's sake?

   _____

4. Reread Scene V, lines 39–55, in which she calls upon the spirits of darkness. What is she asking these spirits to eliminate from her character? What specifically does she ask them to help her do?

   _____

5. What speech to Macbeth in this scene shows that Lady Macbeth is cleverer than he is and more aware of the appearance of things? _____

6. In Scene VI, how does she demonstrate the behavior she suggested to her husband in Scene V? *Clue:* Remember her greetings to Duncan.

   _____

7. In Scene VII, Lady Macbeth demonstrates the strength of her resolution. When Macbeth says he will not go through with the murder, she chides him and accuses him of cowardice. Does she really think he is cowardly? Explain.

   _____

8. In Scene VII, lines 48–59, when Lady Macbeth says she is capable of murder, even of her own child, what is your reaction? Why does she draw such a gruesome parallel to Macbeth's situation (having agreed to kill Duncan and then changing his mind)?

   _____

9. Throughout the planning and execution of the murder, who is the cool, careful mastermind?

   _____

10. What one sign of "weakness" or conscience does Lady Macbeth show in Act II, Scene II?

   _____

11. At this point, what is your opinion of Lady Macbeth? Is she a loving wife, ambitious for her husband, or a coldhearted murderer, or both? Explain your answer on the back of this paper.

Lesson 17: The Importance of Setting in *Macbeth*

Probably you are already aware of the three important elements of a play: the **plot** (what happens), the **setting** (when and where it happens), and the **characters** whose speeches and actions you evaluate to understand why they behave as they do.

The summary of each act will give you a good idea of what happens in *Macbeth*. Lessons 15 and 16 should have made you well acquainted with Macbeth and Lady Macbeth. If you are like most readers, though, you have probably paid little attention to the setting. You already have a simple definition of setting. Broadly speaking, it deals with more than time or place. The playwright creates a certain atmosphere through descriptive passages. The characters he or she creates also reflect moral values of the period. These too are part of the setting. For

example, Macbeth's "vaulting ambition" would have seemed a greater fault to Elizabethan audiences than it does to us. Keep in mind that the Elizabethans were still close to the Medieval attitude that striving for advancement in this world was not important or even desirable; living so as to gain rewards in the afterlife should be one's only aim. Again, to the Elizabethans and to Shakespeare himself, a strong believer in monarchy, murdering a king was a horrible crime. To violate the rules of hospitality was a serious offense in itself. Such moral considerations are all part of the setting of the play.

But now let's review Acts I and II to see how Shakespeare creates the proper atmosphere for his story.

1. In Act I, Scene I, the witches meet in a "desert place" during a thunderstorm. How do the weather and the place contribute to the eerie atmosphere? What color would best symbolize both the setting and the witches?

   _____

2. As Scene II opens in Duncan's battle camp, a sergeant, bloody from his wounds, appears. He tells of "bloody execution" and that Macbeth "unseam'd" his enemy "from the nave to the chaps" and cut off his head. What color best symbolizes this scene? How is that color an appropriate symbol for the play so far?

   _____

3. When Macbeth and Banquo meet the witches on the barren heath, Macbeth mentions the "foul day." Usually, performances of this play show Macbeth and Banquo meeting the witches in a very foggy place. If Macbeth's "foul" means foggy, why is the weather appropriate for what happens? *Clue:* Do Macbeth and Banquo see clearly in any sense? Technically, why would the fog be to the actors' advantage?

   _____

4. Reread Lady Macbeth's speech, Act I, Scene V, lines 39–41. You now can have little doubt of her intentions to kill the king. Why is it appropriate that she mentions the raven in this speech? *Clue:* Remember the raven's color, voice, and reputation.

   _____

5. In Act I, Scene VI, when the king (with Banquo and others) arrives at Macbeth's castle, Banquo mentions that the martlet (martin or swallow), a bird fond of nesting around churches, had made his nest there. Reread his speech, lines 3–9. What is the obvious contrast with the raven that Lady Macbeth mentioned? In view of what you already know of Lady Macbeth's intentions, why is it ironic that Banquo mentions the gentle martin?

   _____

6. See Duncan's speech that opens Act I, Scene VI. Again, what is the irony, or contradiction, here? Note that Shakespeare creates the irony by contrasting what *is* (which we, the readers, know) with what *seems* to be (to Duncan).

   _____

7. Finally, at what time of day or night was Duncan killed? Why was the time well suited to the deed?

   _____

It should now be clear that setting can be used to underline important facts of the plot.

Reading Quiz: *Macbeth,* **Act II**

1. What gift for Lady Macbeth does Duncan entrust to Banquo?

   _____

2. The grooms actually wake just after Macbeth murders the king and while Macbeth is still in the same room with them. What do they do?

   _____

3. Just after he murders the king, what does Macbeth think he hears a voice cry?

   _____

4. Why does Lady Macbeth want her husband to smear the sleeping grooms with Duncan's blood?

   _____

5. While Macduff is in the king's chamber, Lennox talks to Macbeth about the previous night. What does he say took place?

   _____

6. To what countries do Malcolm and Donalbain go?

   _____

7. Is there any indication in the final scene of this act that Macduff is not pleased to see Macbeth crowned? Explain.

   _____

What Happens in Act III, *Macbeth*

Act III, Scene I At the palace, Banquo, alone, gives voice to his thoughts—Macbeth has everything the witches promised, but Banquo suspects that Macbeth is Duncan's murderer. He muses that perhaps the witches' prophecy may come true for him, too, and that he will be the father of kings. Macbeth, Lady Macbeth, and several courtiers come in. Macbeth and Lady Macbeth tell Banquo that he will be their chief guest at the banquet that evening. Macbeth tells Banquo of affairs of state on which he would have asked Banquo's advice if Banquo were not going out for a long ride that afternoon. He complains that Malcolm and Donalbain are in England and Ireland, apparently spreading rumors of some sort. When the others leave, Macbeth asks the servant to show in two men waiting to see him. While he is alone, Macbeth reveals his state of mind. He is uneasy about Banquo and sees him as a threat. Also, it rankles that he has committed murder, has sold his soul to the devil, actually, so that Banquo's descendants, not his own, will reign in Scotland. The murderers come in, and Macbeth talks to them about Banquo. He convinces them that he is an enemy to them and to Macbeth himself. But Macbeth cannot banish Banquo without bringing others' disapproval upon himself. Thus, he needs the murderers. They must kill Banquo and Fleance that very night; he will later give them specific instructions as to the time and place.

Act III, Scene II Lady Macbeth sends a servant to tell Macbeth that she wishes to speak to him. In a brief soliloquy, she reveals that her new status as queen has brought her no contentment since she and Macbeth gained status by "destruction." When Macbeth comes in, she chides him for keeping too much to himself and brooding. She says that what's done must be forgotten. Macbeth says, metaphorically, that they have not succeeded in making their position secure and that it would be better to be dead than to live in fear. Lady Macbeth tells him to put on a cheerful appearance for the night's banquet. He tells her to do the same and to be especially attentive to Banquo, whose friendship they need. He then suggests that Banquo and his son are a threat and

hints of a dark deed to be done, but does not tell his wife exactly what he has in mind.

Act III, Scene III A third murderer, a stranger, joins the other two, saying Macbeth has sent him. It is just after sunset when Banquo and Fleance appear. The murderers attack and kill Banquo, but Fleance escapes.

Act III, Scene IV The banquet begins with Macbeth greeting his guests. The murderers appear at the door, and Macbeth speaks to them. Discovering that only Banquo has been killed, he is at first gravely troubled, then rationalizes that Fleance is no threat at present. Banquo's ghost appears to Macbeth, sitting in the seat he was going to occupy. On seeing the ghost, Macbeth acts so strangely that the lords are alarmed. Lady Macbeth reassures them, saying he has had such fits since childhood. In asides to Macbeth, she tries to calm him and succeeds until the ghost appears a second time. Macbeth's words then are so strange that the guests leave. Macbeth then comments to his wife about Macduff's failure to attend the banquet and says that he will talk to the witches again to learn the future.

Act III, Scene V (This scene was not written by Shakespeare.) Hecate, goddess of the infernal regions, tells the witches that spirits will appear to Macbeth and confuse him.

Act III, Scene VI Lennox and another lord discuss recent events. Lennox is suspicious that Macbeth is Duncan's murderer and the engineer of Banquo's murder. The other lord reports that Malcolm is raising an army in England to challenge Macbeth and that Macduff has gone to England to help him. Both fear for Macduff's safety since he has refused Macbeth's summons.

Lesson 18: Macbeth, "The Secret'st Man of Blood"

As you learned in Lesson 15, one theory of tragedy is that it concerns the downfall or death of an otherwise sympathetic or likeable character whose "fatal flaw" leads to destruction. Macbeth's flaw is obvious enough; it is his "vaulting ambition." One difficulty in applying the "fatal flaw" theory to Macbeth, though, is that it is not clear how much of Macbeth's subsequent behavior results from the witches' prophecy. Part of that prophecy, his gaining the title of Thane of Cawdor, comes true so soon after their weird utterances. Has his ambition already caused him to want Duncan's throne? Is it a chain of circumstances—the prophecy, Duncan's announcement that Malcolm would succeed him, and Lady Macbeth's insistence on her evil plan—that drives Macbeth to kill his guest, the king?

Whatever the causes of the first murder, by Act III, Macbeth admits,

> *I am in blood*
> *Stepp'd in so far that, should I wade no more,*
> *Returning were as tedious as go o'er,*

for he has already arranged for the murder of Banquo and Fleance, and he implies at the end of this act that there are more evil deeds to come.

Answers to the following questions will show you how Macbeth has now changed from an honored conquering hero, a man "too full o' the milk of human kindness," to a ruthless man, trusting no one, a man set on an unchangeable course of terrible destruction.

1. Remember that in Act I, Scene V, before Duncan's murder, Lady Macbeth advises her husband to conceal his thoughts and smile, for his expression is too easily read. Look at Macbeth's conversation with Banquo in Act III, Scene I. What evidence is there that Macbeth has now learned to conceal his thoughts and finds it easier to be hypocritical?

_____

2. In Act III, Scene I, what seemingly innocent question does Macbeth ask Banquo about his son? What is the real reason for the question?

_____

3. In Act III, Scene I, is Macbeth still honest with himself? See lines 48–72.

_____

4. In Act I, Lady Macbeth manipulates Macbeth's mind to convince him to murder Duncan. In Act III, Scene I, how does Macbeth manipulate the murderers' minds?

_____

5. In Act III, what evidence is there that Macbeth now acts independently of Lady Macbeth and that he no longer confides in her?

_____

6. Why doesn't Macbeth tell the truth to his wife?

_____

7. In Scene IV, lines 39–43 and 85–92, after the murderers have reported to Macbeth, how is he hypocritical in his comments to the lords?

_____

8. You have already seen that Macbeth is a man of imagination. How has his imagination become his enemy in Scene IV? See especially his speech in lines 122–126.

_____

9. What evidence is there that Macbeth is now suspicious and crafty?

_____

10. Copy the lines at the end of Scene IV that show that Macbeth now will let nothing stand in his way and that, if necessary, he is ready to embark on a course of evil deeds.

_____

Reading Quiz: *Macbeth,* **Act III**

1. Why does Macbeth want to know whether or not Fleance is going riding with his father in the afternoon, before the banquet?

   _____

   _____

2. What does Macbeth tell the murderers that Banquo has done to them?

   _____

   _____

3. What state of mind do the murderers reveal in their speeches to Macbeth?

   _____

   _____

4. When the ghost appears a second time, and Macbeth's remarks confuse and startle the guests, what does Lady Macbeth do to save the situation?

   _____

   _____

5. How is Macbeth keeping himself aware of the attitudes and activities of the lords of his court?

   _____

   _____

6. What has made Macbeth certain that Macduff is not his friend?

   _____

   _____

What Happens in Act IV, *Macbeth*

Act IV, Scene I In a cave, the three witches are chanting and stirring up an evil brew in a huge cauldron as Macbeth enters. He addresses them, saying that no matter what mischief they do or where they get their knowledge, they must answer his questions. They answer by asking if he would rather hear from them or their "masters." Macbeth says, "let me see 'em." The first apparition, an armed head, advises Macbeth to beware Macduff. The second apparition, a bloody child, counsels Macbeth to be bold and unafraid, "for none of woman born shall harm Macbeth." The third apparition, a crowned child with a tree in its hand, counsels Macbeth to be proud and indifferent to malcontents or conspirators, for Macbeth cannot be conquered "until Great Birnam Wood to high Dunsinane Hill Shall come against him."

Knowing that trees cannot move, Macbeth is happy with the apparition's words. He believes now that his position is secure, but he still wants to know if Banquo's descendants will reign. The witches advise him to seek no more knowledge, but he insists. Then apparitions of eight kings pass before his eyes, with Banquo's ghost following. Macbeth is angry and asks the witches if what he has seen is true. They say it is, dance briefly, and vanish. Lennox appears. Macbeth asks him if he has seen the witches. Of course, he has not. Lennox reports that Macduff has fled to England. Macbeth chides himself that he did not take quicker action against Macduff. He resolves to act immediately on his thoughts and says that he will have Macduff's castle attacked and Lady Macduff and the children killed.

Act IV, Scene II Ross is comforting Lady Macduff, who does not understand why her husband has left so suddenly and considers it desertion. Ross cannot tell her why Macduff has gone but says he acted wisely. Ross counsels patience, saying that things will improve. He then leaves. Lady Macduff and her little son have a conversation. The child seems wise beyond his years. A messenger interrupts them, tells Lady Macduff that she and her children are in danger and should flee, then leaves quickly himself. Lady Macduff is frightened and does not know where she should go. Almost immediately, the murderers come in, looking for Macduff and calling him traitor. When the boy tries to defend his father's name, the murderers stab him, then run after Lady Macduff, who is trying to escape.

Act IV, Scene III Macduff, in England with Malcolm, tells him the sorry state that Scotland is in. At first, Malcolm seems not to trust Macduff, fearing a trap set by Macbeth, but soon he has no doubt of Macduff's sincerity. To test Macduff, Malcolm says that should he himself become king, he has more faults than Macbeth, and he lists them. Macduff despairs for Scotland, but then Malcolm admits that he has been merely testing Macduff's loyalty. He says Siward has already raised an army of 10,000 men to challenge Macbeth, and he asks Macduff to join him and Siward. Ross appears and talks first of the sorry state of Scotland, but Macduff asks him for more personal news of his wife and children. At first, Ross says only that they were at peace when he left them. Finally, he tells Macduff that his wife, children, even his servants, have been murdered. Malcolm's immediate reaction is that Macduff should take revenge. Macduff, stunned, blames himself, realizing that they were killed in his place. Finally, he says that he will seek out Macbeth and take his revenge. Malcolm says that they will go immediately to King Edward and then depart for Scotland.

Albert Finney as Macbeth

© 1985, 2000 J. Weston Walch, Publisher   *51*   *The Complete Guide to Shakespeare's Best Plays*

Name _____ Date _____

Lesson 19: What Qualities Suit a King?

Scholars believe that Shakespeare wrote *Macbeth* in 1606. Thus, it came in the reign of Queen Elizabeth's successor, James I, who ascended the throne in 1603. It is speculated that the play was written at James's request, for it was believed that James's royal descent was from Fleance, son of Banquo, and that in the person of James the royal houses of England and Scotland were united. Such a political union was exactly what the king hoped for. Early in his reign, he brought up the matter of a Scottish union with England, but the English parliament was not enthusiastic about the idea.

The historical background for the play came from Holinshed's *Chronicles*, which was also Shakespeare's source for his English history plays.

In *Macbeth*, Shakespeare combined Holinshed's accounts of the reigns of several Scottish kings. However loosely he interpreted history, Shakespeare (a strong monarchist and loyal subject) drew a clear picture of the qualities of an ideal king, contrasting those qualities with the ones a usurper (a person who wrongfully takes) such as Macbeth possessed. In making a strong case for orderly succession and portraying the rightful monarchs (Duncan, Edward the Confessor, and Malcolm) as men of modesty and virtue, Shakespeare could not help but please James I.

It is in Act IV that Shakespeare is most specific in outlining kingly qualities, but some earlier scenes also give clues to what he admired in a ruler.

1. Look first at Macbeth's speech in Act I, Scene VII, lines 16–20. What does he say typified Duncan as king?

   _____

2. In the opening scene of the play, what qualities does Duncan reveal in each of the following instances?

   A. his treatment of the sergeant who brought news of the battle

   _____

   B. his treatment of Macbeth, the military hero

   _____

   C. his announcing that Malcolm will succeed him

   _____

   D. his arrival at Macbeth's castle and meeting Lady Macbeth

   _____

3. In Act IV, Scene III, Malcolm is testing Macduff and pretends to possess a number of unfavorable qualities. See his speeches in lines 50 through 99. What are these qualities? Which does Macbeth possess?

   _____

4. In his speech beginning with line 91, he also lists the "king-becoming" graces. What are they?

   _____

5. Reread Malcolm's speech beginning with line 146. What special gifts or qualities of Edward the Confessor does he describe?

   _____

6. See Malcolm's last speech (also the last speech of the play). What will be his first concerns as king? What do these concerns show about him as a king and an administrator?

   _____

7. Shakespeare reveals in several of his plays his strong belief that if a rightful ruler is deposed or killed, only chaos can result. State briefly how events in *Macbeth* emphasize that point.

   _____

Reading Quiz: *Macbeth,* Act IV

1. Name any three of the many ingredients in the witches' brew.

   _____

   _____

2. After the second apparition (the bloody child) appears, what resolve does Macbeth make concerning Macduff?

   _____

   _____

3. After Ross leaves, what prompts Lady Macduff to say to her son that his father is dead when actually he is not?

   _____

   _____

4. What are two of the faults of which Malcolm accuses himself to test Macduff?

   _____

   _____

5. Malcolm speaks of his host, the English king, Edward the Confessor. What great gift of Edward's does Malcolm describe?

   _____

   _____

Lesson 20: Macbeth and the Supernatural

In no other of Shakespeare's plays does the supernatural seem the powerful, ever-present force that it does in *Macbeth*. And in no other of his plays is the **protagonist** (main character) more receptive to psychic or otherworldly events than is the sensitive and imaginative Macbeth.

Some modern Shakespearean critics, applying twentieth-century psychology to this seventeenth-century play, have been able to remove much of the mystery and power from Shakespeare's witches and apparitions. To them, the witches are simply old hags, sneaking around the battlefield, picking up bits of information and combining them with lucky guesses. The ghostly figures are figments of Macbeth's feverish imagination, and their accurate prophecies are merely coincidence. But Elizabethan audiences, like Macbeth himself, would have had little doubt of the witches' authenticity. Hadn't King James himself written *Daemonologie*, encouraging the persecution and punishment of witches? Elizabethan audiences would have realized too that Macbeth, in seeking to know the future (the unknowable), was committing a grave sin and joining with the powers of darkness.

As for Lady Macbeth, her terrible invocation to the "murdering ministers" in Act I is answered in succeeding scenes by the spirits of evil who make her an instrument of destruction. Eventually, they destroy her too, for the hideousness of the crime she and Macbeth have committed preys on her mind, causing her to lose her reason and eventually take her own life.

Let's trace the supernatural influences in Macbeth's life, from his first meeting the witches.

1. Aside from spurring Macbeth's ambition, what effect does the witches' prophecy have on his relationship with Banquo, and what effect does it have later on Banquo himself? (See his soliloquy that opens Act III, Scene 1).

   _____

2. What eventual effect does Macbeth's encounter with the witches have on his relationship with Lady Macbeth? _____

3. Reread Macbeth's soliloquy in Act II, Scene I, lines 33–64. How does Macbeth attempt to explain his vision of the dagger to himself? _____

4. In lines 49–64 of that speech, how does Macbeth imaginatively express his sense of all-pervading evil?

   _____

5. In Scene II, how do you explain the voice that Macbeth heard cry, "Sleep no more! Macbeth does murder sleep." Did the voice make an accurate prediction of Macbeth's future?

   _____

6. In Act III, Scene I, lines 68—69, what is the "eternal jewel" that Macbeth has given to "the common enemy of man"? Who is that enemy? By what act did Macbeth give his "eternal jewel"?

   _____

7. The third murderer in Act III, Scene III, is not identified. It is sometimes suggested that he is Macbeth himself. Why does that explanation seem illogical? Who could he possibly be?

   _____

8. What might be a modern explanation of Macbeth's seeing Banquo's ghost? What is the effect of its appearance on the lords, even though they don't see it? Why is that effect to Macbeth's disadvantage?

   _____

9. When Macbeth consults the witches, which apparition angers him? Which give him a false sense of security? How do the apparitions confuse him, as Hecate has promised they would?

   _____

10. Do you see any possible explanation of Lady Macduff's mysterious visitor? _____

    Do you see the difficulties in deciding whether Macbeth is a man in conflict with evil within himself or a man beset by and eventually destroyed by the powers of darkness?

What Happens in Act V, *Macbeth*

Act V, Scene I One of Lady Macbeth's gentle-women reports to a doctor that the queen has taken to walking and talking in her sleep, but the woman will not repeat what Lady Macbeth says. At that moment, Lady Macbeth appears, sleep-walking. She goes through the motions of wash-ing her hands, an action the gentlewoman explains that she often does for as much as fifteen minutes. Lady Macbeth's monologue refers unmistakably to blood and to Duncan's, Lady Macduff's, and Banquo's deaths. The doctor and gentlewoman realize the cause of Lady Macbeth's torment but dare not speak their thoughts. The doctor says that Lady Macbeth needs God's help, not his, and advises the woman to watch her and keep her from bodily harm.

Act V, Scene II Near Macbeth's castle at Dunsi-nane, Menteith tells the other nobles that the English forces, with Siward, Malcolm, and Macduff, are close by. Angus says that the army these nobles lead will join the English forces near Birnam Wood. Caithness reports that Macbeth is fortifying the castle. Some say Macbeth is mad; others that he is in a fury but that he has no loyal supporters. The nobles depart to join Malcolm.

Act V, Scene III For courage, Macbeth is repeating the words of the apparitions when a servant reports the approach of 10,000 English soldiers. Calling the servant cowardly, Macbeth dismisses him. An officer, Seyton, confirms the servant's report, and Macbeth decides to put on his armor. A doctor reports that Lady Macbeth's mind is very troubled. When Macbeth asks if he cannot cure that, the doctor says that it is something the patient must cure. Macbeth then tells the doctor that the thanes are deserting him and wishes the doctor could cure Scotland's ills and rid her of English troops. In an aside, the doctor wishes he were someplace else.

Act V, Scene IV Malcolm, Siward, Macduff, and the other Scottish nobles are near Birnam Wood. For camouflage, Malcolm suggests that each soldier cut a large branch from a tree and carry it before him so that they can get closer to the enemy before being detected.

Act V, Scene V Macbeth tells Seyton to hang out the castle banners and await the attack. He is certain that the castle cannot be taken. The wail-ing of women within the castle has little effect on Macbeth, who, by his own admission, has "supp'd full with horrors." Then word comes that Lady Macbeth is dead. Macbeth's next speech, lines 17–28, expresses his world-weariness and despair. A messenger comes in to report a strange phenome-non; Birnam Wood seems to be advancing on Dunsinane Castle. Macbeth remembers the appa-rition's words and prepares to fight despite his mood of hopelessness.

Act V, Scene VI Now that they are near enough to the castle, Malcolm tells his forces to throw down their branches. Then he sends his forces into battle.

Act V, Scene VII Young Siward, who has come with his father's troops, encounters Macbeth. When he realizes who his opponent is, he attacks fiercely, but Macbeth slays him. Meanwhile, Macduff searches for Macbeth, determined to kill him. Malcolm and old Siward exchange a few words. The battle is going well for them.

Act V, Scene VIII Apparently, Macbeth has consid-ered suicide and rejected the idea. When Macduff comes upon him, Macbeth is reluctant to fight him, saying that he has taken too much of Macduff's blood already and that he is invulnera-ble to one of woman born. Yet he will not yield to Macduff, lest he be captured and scorned. They fight; meanwhile, Malcolm and Siward have been victorious, but Siward's son is missing. Ross comes in and tells Siward that his son has died a hero's death. His father says he could ask no more. Macduff appears, carrying Macbeth's head, and hails Malcolm as King of Scotland. Malcolm promises the nobles rewards, saying that he will recall the exiles who fled Macbeth and punish those who did Macbeth's evil deeds for him.

Lesson 21: Examining the Themes in *Macbeth*

In addition to following the plot, understanding the characters, and visualizing the setting, one thing more is required of a reader if he or she is to appreciate a play or novel. The reader must be aware of the themes (central ideas) that the author is illustrating through the events of the plot. For example, in *Romeo and Juliet*, Shakespeare's theme is that "the course of true love never did run smooth" (that's a quotation from another of his plays, *A Midsummer Night's Dream*).

In *Julius Caesar*, one of Shakespeare's themes is that if the rightful ruler is deposed or killed, chaos results. In *Macbeth*, Shakespeare again shows that violence begets violence. Perhaps the play's most emphasized theme is that an excess of ambition can make a man ruthless in his search for power. Also, through Macbeth's actions, Shakespeare shows that absolute power makes one evil.

Let's look now at incidents in the play that illustrate each of these themes.

1. After the death of Duncan, what happens to Macbeth's mind? to Lady Macbeth's?

    _____

2. What is the ultimate effect of Duncan's death on Banquo? on Macduff?

    _____

3. From various speakers, what do you learn is the effect of Duncan's death on Scotland in general?

    _____

4. The play ends on a positive note (see Malcolm's final speech). Why is it positive?

    _____

5. Another English poet, Alexander Pope, once wrote:

    > *Vice* is a monster of so frightful mien,***
    > *As to be hated needs but to be seen;*
    > *Yet seen too oft, familiar with her face,*
    > *We first endure, then pity, then embrace.*

    *evil
    **appearance

    Apply these lines to the change in Macbeth's character. Use the back of this paper if necessary.

    _____

6. Since Macbeth was so reluctant to kill Duncan, why did he continue to have murders committed?

    _____

7 How had power made him evil?

    _____

8. Which do you see as the most important theme in the play? Explain.

    _____

    _____

Name_____ Date_____

Lesson 22: Shakespeare's Poetry in *Macbeth*

Shakespeare's plays were written in blank verse. Although he was not the first to use it, no one used blank verse more skillfully. Let's take time to review what **blank verse** is. Briefly defined, it is unrhymed iambic pentameter, but let's break that definition down a bit. An *iamb* is a poetic measure called a **foot**. It is made up of two syllables, with the accent on the second. The word *today* is a perfect iamb. *Penta*, from the Greek, means five, and *meter* refers to the rhythmic pattern of a poem (in this case a five-measure line). Putting it all together, an iambic pentameter line has five feet, each foot (iamb) having two syllables, with the accent or beat on the second. It might be diagrammed like this:

Todáy/ Todáy/ Todáy/ Todáy/ Todáy
  1   2   3   4   5

Look at this iambic pentameter line from *Macbeth*, Act II, Scene I, line 2:

The moón/ is dowń;/ I havé/ not heard/ the clock.
    1   2   3   4   5

1. Now you try one. Divide the following line into five iambic feet and mark the accented syllables. (Remember to work with syllables, not necessarily whole words.)

   Away and mark the time with fairest show . . .

   In Shakespeare's plays, rhymed iambic pentameter lines sometimes appear at the end of a scene. For example, the line following the one you just scanned is:

   False face must hide what the false heart doth know.

   These two rhyming lines end Act I, Scene VII. One theory is that Shakespeare used rhyme to close a scene because actors waiting to go on stage could learn or hear the rhymed lines more easily and would appear on cue. Studying the mechanics of Shakespeare's poetry helps you to appreciate his technical skill. A more rewarding exercise is analyzing the poetic devices and the word choices that make his lines so memorable. This is why he is the most-quoted poet in the English language.

2. Look now at what is probably the most famous speech in *Macbeth*: Act V, Scene V, Macbeth's lines 19–28, beginning "To morrow, and tomorrow, and tomorrow." Note that *tomorrow* is repeated three times. What is the effect of this deliberate repetition? (Read this and the following line aloud. You will see that they cannot be read quickly.)

   _____

3. Look at Shakespeare's choice of verbs in these lines:
   Creeps _____ struts _____ frets _____
   Can you substitute other verbs that would convey the idea as effectively, without resorting to adverbs? Try it.

4. You will remember that both metaphors and similes are comparisons. In a metaphor, the comparison is implied: *Jenny Lind was a Swedish nightingale.* In a simile, the comparison is stated with *like* or *as: Jenny Lind sang like a bird*. What four metaphors for *life* does Shakespeare use in lines 19–28?

   _____

   Are there any similes? _____

5. Beginning with "it is a tale . . .," paraphrase the last three lines of the speech.

   _____

   Do you see that Shakespeare's way of making the statement is more dramatic than your prose line?

6. Reread Macbeth's opening speech in Act I, Scene VII, and list any similes it contains.

   _____

   Finally, reread Macbeth's speech in Act IV, Scene I, lines 52–61. Note the series of clauses, each beginning with *though* and each having the same grammatical structure. This kind of repetition, called **parallel structure**, is used often by writers and speakers to gain emphasis. It was a favorite device in both Lincoln's and John F. Kennedy's speeches.

Reading Quiz: *Macbeth*, **Act V**

1 In Lady Macbeth's famous sleepwalking speech, to what does she refer in this line?
Out, damned spot! out, I say!

_____

_____

2. As the English army approaches, what two prophecies of the apparitions does Macbeth repeat to himself?

_____

_____

3. How does Malcolm's tactic of having his soldiers cut branches for camouflage tie in with the apparition's prophecy?

_____

_____

4. Why, in Macbeth's words, does he wait for the English forces rather than taking the offensive and going out to meet them?

_____

_____

5. Why does Macduff say that he will kill only Macbeth, not any of his soldiers?

_____

_____

6. Why didn't the apparition's prophecy that "none of woman born shall harm Macbeth" apply to Macduff?

_____

_____

7. According to Malcolm's final speech, how did Lady Macbeth die?

_____

_____

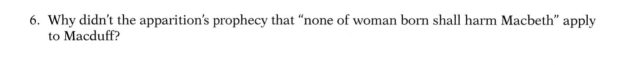

Name _____ Date _____

Final Test: *Macbeth*

Complete the following sentences in the fewest possible words.

1. The witches promise Macbeth that he will be _____ and _____.
2. They promise Banquo that he will _____.
3. Lady Macbeth calls upon the "murdering ministers" to help her to _____.
4. To assure an orderly succession, Duncan names _____ to become the next king.
5. After killing the king, Macbeth hears a voice say that "Macbeth does murder" _____.
6. Malcolm and Donalbain flee from Macbeth's castle after their father's murder because _____.
7. Macduff reveals his dislike or distrust of Macbeth when he refuses to go to see _____.
8. Because Lady Macduff does not know why her husband went to England, she is angry and calls him a

   _____.
9. Birnam Wood comes to Dunsinane when _____.
10. The apparition's prophecy did not apply to Macduff because he was not _____.
11. The man who clearly contrasts with Macbeth because he is loyal and selfless, putting Scotland's welfare ahead of his own, is _____.
12. Macbeth's greatest fault was his _____.

Define each of the following terms from the drama:

13. A. soliloquy _____ B. aside _____
    C. protagonist _____ D. comic relief* _____
    *Remember the porter going to answer the knock.

Who is the speaker in each of the following quotations?

14. *Tomorrow, and tomorrow, and tomorrow,*
    Creeps in this petty pace from day to day,
    To the last syllable of recorded time;   _____

15. *Out, damned spot! out, I say!*   _____

16. *He has no children. All my pretty ones?*
    Did you say all? O hell-kite! All?   _____

17. *It is myself I mean: in whom I know*
    All the particulars of vice so grafted
    That, when they shall be open'd, black Macbeth
    Will seem as pure as snow,   _____

18. *Had he not resembled*
    My father as he slept, I had done't.   _____

19. What time of night is being described below?
    The moon is down. . . . There's husbandry* in heaven;   *economy
    There candles are all out.

20. Whose castle is described in these lines?   _____
    This castle has a pleasant seat; the air
    Nimbly and sweetly recommends itself
    Unto our gentle senses.

21. In view of later events, Banquo's description of the castle and its peaceful setting becomes ironic. Why?

    _____

    _____

To the Teacher:

Suggestions for Presenting *Hamlet*

Sources

It is possible that Shakespeare was influenced by an English trend of the late 1500's and early 1600's to revive older "tragedies of blood," which often had revenge as their theme. A play called *Hamlet* had been performed in London in 1589 and again in 1594. (Shakespeare's *Hamlet* was probably not written until 1599 at the earliest.) Actually, the Hamlet story was known to exist in Scandinavia as early as the tenth century. Various other versions appeared over the years, but it remained for Shakespeare to create in his tragic hero Hamlet a character who has fascinated playgoers ever since.

Topics for Class Discussion

Have a few students consult an encyclopedia or other reference to find out what they can about the interests and accomplishments of Queen Elizabeth I. They should then report to the class. Have them ask their classmates what they know about the present queen of England, Elizabeth II. Does she have any characteristics in common with her predecessor?

A group of students could investigate the four elements and four humors that "determined" a person's disposition. They will need to check an encyclopedia or the Internet under *Medieval Medicine*. Ask them to decide what humor was predominant in Hamlet, in Fortinbras. They should report their findings and opinions to the class. They could ask their classmates to suggest certain public figures of today who would seem to fit into each category.

As students read the play on their own, ask them to list expressions they have heard before—for example, "Something is rotten in the state of Denmark." Have them compare lists in class.

Topics for Oral Reports

A small group of students could look for a description and picture of the Globe theater. They should investigate (and report on) how certain effects were created on stage. For example, how would the ghost's appearance in *Hamlet* have been managed? (Marchette Chute's *Shakespeare of London* is a good source for this exercise.)

Ask a group of students to do some research on the language of the flowers mentioned by Shakespeare. They should investigate the Elizabethan symbolism for such common flowers as the rose and the lily. Another group could consult an herbal (a book about herbs and plants) and find out the supposed medicinal properties of certain herbs—especially borage and yarrow. Both groups should report their findings to the class.

Hands-On Activities

From a seed catalog, a few students could clip illustrations of the flowers Ophelia mentions in Act IV, Scene V. Then they could make a poster, using Ophelia's words beneath each picture—for example, "There's rosemary, that's for remembrance."

Ask some students to make a poster advertising a performance of *Hamlet* at the Globe. Have them mention the time, the exact location, and the admission price. They should give billing to the leading actor, and give a very brief summary of the play (for example, "*Hamlet*, a play about . . ."). Marchette Chute's *Shakespeare of London* is a good source of information.

Vocabulary Building

In their notebooks, students should collect at least two unfamiliar words from each scene of the play, avoiding words that are footnoted. They should look up each word in a dictionary, define it, and write a sentence using it. In class, students can compare notes and learn from one another's work.

What Happens in Act I, *Hamlet*

Act I, Scene I It is midnight and bitter cold. On a platform (a level space on the battlements) outside the castle at Elsinore in Denmark, a sentry, or guard (Francisco), is being relieved by another (Bernardo). Later, Marcellus and Horatio join Bernardo. Horatio is there at Marcellus's request but doubts the sentries' story that on two previous nights they have seen a ghost. But the ghost reappears, and Horatio, seeing its resemblance to the dead king, Hamlet, asks it to speak. Instead, it stalks away.

Horatio interprets the ghost's appearance as an omen that something strange is about to happen in Denmark. He tells the sentries that Fortinbras, a young, hot-headed Norwegian, has gathered an army and intends to march on Denmark to take back the lands that his father, King Fortinbras, lost to King Hamlet.

The ghost then reappears. Again, Horatio faces it and asks it to speak. Before it can, a rooster crows, signaling the dawn, and the ghost retreats once more. Horatio and the others agree that Prince Hamlet must be told of the night's happenings.

Act I, Scene II King Claudius is carrying out state business. (Claudius, brother of the dead king, Hamlet, has succeeded him to the throne. He has married the widow, Queen Gertrude, Prince Hamlet's mother.) In an attempt to avoid combat with Fortinbras, Claudius is sending messengers, Cornelius and Voltimand, to the elderly king of Norway. He wants to inform him of his headstrong nephew's (Fortinbras') intention to wage war against Denmark. Next, Laertes, son of Claudius's trusted elderly counselor, Polonius, asks permission to return to France now that Claudius's coronation is over.

Having granted Laertes' request, Claudius turns to Hamlet, his nephew (now his stepson). Claudius says that he and the queen are troubled to see Hamlet still grieving over his father's death. Claudius asks Hamlet to accept him as his new father and assures Hamlet that he will be the successor to the throne. He and Gertrude entreat Hamlet to remain at court rather than resume his studies at Wittenberg.

After everyone else leaves, Hamlet reveals that he is depressed almost to the point of suicide. His anger and disgust are directed toward his mother because so soon after his father's death, she has married a man inferior to King Hamlet in every way. Bernardo and Marcellus join Hamlet and tell him of the previous night's event. He resolves to watch with them this night.

Act I, Scene III In Polonius's house, Laertes and his sister, Ophelia, are saying good-bye. Laertes warns her against Hamlet, saying that a prince must choose his wife carefully and that Hamlet is probably not seriously interested in her. At that moment, Polonius comes in and gives Laertes some fatherly advice about what his behavior should be in France. When he finds out that they have been talking about Hamlet, he adds his opinion that Hamlet is probably amusing himself with Ophelia. He tells her to avoid Hamlet. She says she will obey.

Act I, Scene IV At midnight, Hamlet, Horatio, and Marcellus are on the platform, wondering if the ghost will appear. It does, and although Hamlet is not certain if it is his dead father or an evil spirit, he speaks to it. He asks why it has returned from the tomb. The ghost does not answer but beckons Hamlet to follow it. Horatio and Marcellus beg him not to, but he does follow the ghost.

Act I, Scene V When they are alone, the ghost tells Hamlet that if he loved his father, he must avenge his father's murder. The ghost (King Hamlet) describes how his brother, Claudius, murdered him, then took his throne and queen. Although offended that Gertrude remarried so soon after his death, he warns Hamlet to take no revenge on her. Her guilty conscience will punish her enough. Because it is almost dawn, the ghost then disappears. Hamlet does not tell the others what the ghost has said but makes them promise to tell no one what they have seen.

Statue of Hamlet, at Stratford-on-Avon

Lesson 23: Getting Acquainted with the Characters

To understand *Hamlet*, you must be able to follow the action (the plot). You must imagine the setting (when and where the action takes place). Above all, you must get acquainted with the characters—their physical appearance, the ways they behave, and their reasons for behaving as they do. As you read the play, you will actually listen in on their conversations. A **soliloquy** (a speech made by an actor who is alone on the stage) can even let you know what the character is thinking.

Answering the following questions will help you decide how familiar you have already become with some of the major characters.

1. In Scene I, Horatio, a sensible and practical man, doubts Marcellus's and Bernardo's ghost story until he sees the apparition himself. After its appearance, how does he show that he too believes in ghosts?

   _____

2. When the ghost reappears, what does Horatio do that shows his courage (lines 126–127)?

   _____

3. In Scene II, you meet Claudius, the new king of Denmark. What two actions does he take that show he is an able administrator?

   _____

4. Why is Claudius so pleased when he believes that Hamlet intends to stay at court rather than return to the university?

   _____

5. When Hamlet is alone in Scene II, line 129, he begins his first soliloquy, "O that this too too solid flesh would melt." Describe briefly his state of mind.

   _____

6. In Scene III, both Polonius and Laertes are suspicious of Hamlet's intentions toward Ophelia. Since they have nothing on which to base their suspicions, what conclusions might you draw about their own attitudes toward women? (*Clue:* See Ophelia's reply to Laertes' advice, lines 45–51.)

   _____

7. In Scene IV, what reasons does Hamlet give for being unafraid to follow the ghost? (*Clue:* See lines 64–68.)

   _____

   How does this speech reinforce the statement Hamlet made in the soliloquy referred to in question 5?

   _____

8. At the end of Act I, without revealing what the ghost has said, Hamlet swears his friends to secrecy. He tells them that if his behavior is strange in the future, they must pretend that they do not know why. Why does he decide to act like a madman?

   _____

9. Before he knows how or by whom his father was murdered, Hamlet has already said he will take swift revenge. In his final speech in Act I, how has his attitude changed slightly, and how do you account for the change?

   _____

10. How old do you think Hamlet is, and what do you think he looks like? Explain what lines in the play have given you these impressions.

   _____

Name _____ Date _____

Reading Quiz: *Hamlet,* Act I

1. Why is the cock's crow important in the opening scene of the play?

   _____

   _____

2. When Hamlet hears of his father's ghost from Marcellus and Horatio, what is his immediate suspicion?

   _____

   _____

3. What caution does he give to Horatio, Macellus, and Bernardo?

   _____

   _____

4. State briefly Polonius's advice to Laertes about either A or B.

   A. his clothing _____

   _____

   B. friendships _____

   _____

5. What custom of the Danes does Hamlet say gives them a poor reputation in other nations?

   _____

   _____

6. According to King Hamlet's ghost, how did Claudius murder him?

   _____

   _____

7. While Hamlet is swearing his friends to secrecy after the ghost's appearance, what is happening at the same time?

   _____

   _____

What Happens in Act II, *Hamlet*

Act II, Scene I Polonius is sending a servant, Reynaldo, to France to spy on Laertes and see how he is behaving. Polonius tells Reynaldo to talk to Laertes' acquaintances, pretending to know him slightly, and to suggest that he is immoral. Thus, Polonius tells Reynaldo, he can trick people into telling whatever they know about Laertes's behavior.

Reynaldo leaves. Ophelia comes in, excited and troubled because Hamlet has just visited her, acting very strange and nervous. He never spoke but studied her face for a long time, then sighed and left her. Polonius interprets this behavior as an indication that Hamlet's love for Ophelia has driven him mad, since Ophelia has been avoiding Hamlet as instructed by Polonius. Polonius decides that he has misjudged Hamlet and that King Claudius must be told how matters stand.

Act II, Scene II Just as Polonius has arranged to have Reynaldo spy on Laertes, King Claudius has summoned two old friends of Hamlet, Rosencrantz and Guildenstern, to spy on Hamlet. He tells them to spend time with Hamlet and try to discover what troubles him. Queen Gertrude also entreats them to find out what is on Hamlet's mind, promising them that they will be well paid for their efforts.

Polonius brings in Voltimand and Cornelius, who have just returned with the good news that the king of Norway has made Fortinbras promise never to take up arms against Denmark. The king does request, though, that Fortinbras be allowed to take his army across Denmark, for he now intends to do battle with the Poles.

In his long-winded way, Polonius then begins to tell Claudius and Gertrude that he has discovered the cause of Hamlet's strange behavior. He is in love with Ophelia, and since she has rejected him (obeying Polonius's order), Hamlet has begun to act like a madman. To prove his point, Polonius proposes to set a trap for Hamlet. He will arrange to have Ophelia meet Hamlet "accidentally." The king and Polonius will conceal themselves behind a wall hanging and listen in on Hamlet's conversation with Ophelia.

At that point, Hamlet appears, completely absorbed in a book that he is reading as he walks. Polonius asks Claudius and Gertrude to leave him alone with Hamlet so he can see what is on Hamlet's mind. Hamlet's answers to his questions make Polonius more certain that Hamlet is crazy. Actually, Hamlet is baiting Polonius; after Polonius leaves, Hamlet calls him a "tedious old fool."

Rosencrantz and Guildenstern arrive and begin to question Hamlet, trying to prove their suspicion that Hamlet's strange behavior is a result of disappointed ambition because he did not inherit the throne from his father. Hamlet outwits them and shows that he is aware that they have come because the king and queen sent for them. When they admit that he is right, he tells them how disillusioned he feels. Nothing in life gives him pleasure.

Rosencrantz and Guildenstern tell Hamlet that they passed some actors coming to perform at court. Polonius comes in and tells Hamlet what he already knows, the news about the players (actors). Again, Hamlet makes fun of Polonius, but Polonius takes no offense since he is so certain that Hamlet is crazy.

Hamlet greets the players and reminds them of a scene from a play he once saw them perform. He begins a speech he remembers, and the first player picks it up where Hamlet stops. Then Hamlet tells Polonius to take the players to their quarters and to treat them kindly. The first player lingers. Hamlet asks him if he knows a play called *The Murder of Gonzago*. When the player says he does, Hamlet requests it for the next night's performance and tells the player that he will write twelve or sixteen lines to be added to the play. He then dismisses the player and Rosencrantz and Guildenstern. Then in a soliloquy, Hamlet scolds himself for not yet having avenged his father's murder. Still troubled by the possibility that the ghost is an evil spirit, not his dead father, Hamlet has decided to test Claudius. He will have the players perform a murder scene. If his uncle acts guilty, Hamlet will have his proof and take his revenge.

Lesson 24: Taking a Closer Look at the Play

We can read *Hamlet* in many ways. First of all, it is a play about murder and revenge. A jealous and ambitious man kills his brother to obtain his crown and his wife. The murdered man's son resolves to take revenge on his father's killer. When and how he will take that revenge becomes the subject of the play.

Looked at in another way, *Hamlet* is a play about two enemies, Hamlet and Claudius, one an intellectual who lives by his ideals; the other a clever and merciless man, willing to use any means to get and keep what he wants. *Hamlet* then becomes a psychological drama, a study of men's minds.

On still another level, the play emphasizes the difficulty Hamlet has in distinguishing illusion (what seems to be) from reality (what is). Hamlet is uncertain as to what he can believe, and his uncertainty is one all human beings face at one time or another.

But more simply, *Hamlet* is a study of family relationships—Prince Hamlet's relationship with his dead father, his mother, and his uncle, the king. His family's destiny is intertwined with that of another family—Claudius's Lord Chamberlain, Polonius, and his son and daughter, Laertes and Ophelia.

Answering the following questions will make you more aware of Shakespeare's emphasis on the problem of illusion versus reality. It will also help you to evaluate the quality of the relationships in the two families.

1. Reread Polonius's advice to Laertes (Act I, Scene III, lines 55–81). Having sent his son off with so much good advice, why would Polonius think it necessary to send someone to check up on him?

_____

2. What do you think of his way of checking up on Laertes?

_____

3. In his instructions to Rosencrantz and Guildenstern, Claudius seems genuinely concerned for Hamlet's welfare. Reread his opening speech in Act II, Scene II. Do you find anything to indicate that he is suspicious of Hamlet?

_____

4. Who seems more willing to accept Polonius's explanation of Hamlet's madness, Gertrude or Claudius? On what do you base your answer?

_____

5. Why do you think Hamlet's mother makes no protest when Polonius suggests listening in on Hamlet and Ophelia?

_____

6. Which is more important to Polonius, his daughter's happiness or maintaining a good relationship with the king and queen? How do you know?

_____

7. In his speech to Rosencrantz and Guildenstern in Act II, Scene II, lines 304–324, Hamlet contrasts how the world is with how it seems to him. Why does it seem that way?

_____

8. Hamlet is impressed that the First Player, who is simply acting a part, has effectively portrayed a highly emotional state. How does Hamlet plan to use the play (an illusion of reality) to determine what is really true?

_____

9. Since the ghost has already explained how and by whom he was murdered, why does Hamlet seek further proof of his uncle's guilt?

_____

Reading Quiz: *Hamlet,* Act II

1. What does Polonius have Reynaldo take to Laertes?

   _____

   _____

2. In Queen Gertrude's opinion, what are the two reasons for Hamlet's melancholy?

   _____

   _____

3. What reply does Claudius give to the king of Norway's request that Fortinbras be allowed to march through Denmark to attack the Poles?

   _____

   _____

4. How does Queen Gertrude show her impatience with Polonius's long-winded speeches?

   _____

   _____

5. Why have the players left the city to travel the countryside and perform where they can?

   _____

   _____

6. At the end of Act II, why does Hamlet scold himself when he is finally alone on the stage?

   _____

   _____

Name _____ Date _____

What Happens in Act III, *Hamlet*

Act III, Scene I With Polonius and Ophelia present, Rosencrantz and Guildenstern report to the king and queen that they have failed to find the cause of Hamlet's strange behavior. When they leave, Claudius asks Gertrude to leave too, for he and Polonius are about to listen in on Hamlet's conversation with Ophelia. After the queen leaves, Polonius instructs his daughter to pretend to read her prayer book. He generalizes that by such pious pretending people often conceal evil actions. His remark troubles Claudius, who has much to conceal himself.

Hamlet comes in, talking to himself about suicide. He says that because life is so difficult, people might use suicide as an escape if they were not held back by fear of what might happen after death. Hamlet then sees and greets Ophelia. She tries to return the gifts he once gave her, but he denies the giving. He is harsh to her, saying, "I did love you once." He talks cynically of marriage and women, then leaves her. Poor Ophelia grieves to see him so changed and, like her father, is certain he is mad.

Having heard the conversation, Claudius doubts that Hamlet is mad but believes he is a threat. He decides to send him to England. Polonius still thinks Hamlet is lovesick and suggests that Gertrude sound him out. Polonius will listen in on their conversation.

Act III, Scene II After instructing the players about their performance, Hamlet talks to Horatio, praising his even temper and sound judgment. He then tells Horatio his plan to test the king. They agree that they will both watch Claudius to see if he acts guilty when the stage murder takes place.

Just before the play, the members of the court come in. Instead of sitting with his mother as she asks, Hamlet sits beside Ophelia, a better place

from which to watch the king. Hamlet is playing the madman again and continues his cynical remarks to Ophelia. In the play, the actress-queen vows eternal love for her husband and says that should he die, she would never remarry. She then leaves the actor-king, who falls asleep. The wicked nephew comes in and pours poison into his ears. Hamlet comments on the play, saying that later the wicked nephew marries the king's wife. Claudius gets up abruptly to leave, and the rest of the court follow. Hamlet now has the proof of guilt he needs.

Rosencrantz and Guildenstern come in to tell Hamlet that the king is ill and that his mother wants to see him. Polonius appears and repeats the summons. They all leave. Hamlet, in a soliloquy, says he will speak harshly to his mother but do her no bodily harm.

Act III, Scene III On the pretext that mad Hamlet is a threat to him, Claudius asks Rosencrantz and Guildenstern to take his nephew to England. Polonius then reports that Hamlet is on his way to his mother's room, where Polonius will listen in on the conversation between mother and son. Alone at last, Claudius tries to pray but cannot. He acknowledges to himself that he cannot pray for forgiveness while he keeps the rewards his evil deed brought him—the crown and Gertrude. Claudius does not see Hamlet come in. Finding his uncle alone and kneeling, Hamlet's first impulse is to kill him. Then he realizes that if he kills Claudius at prayer, his soul may go to Heaven. Hamlet decides to wait.

Act III, Scene IV Hamlet is so harsh to his mother that she fears for her life and cries out. Hidden behind the wall hanging, Polonius shouts, too. Hamlet thinks he hears the king, and he slashes the hanging, killing Polonius. Hamlet realizes from Gertrude's replies to his accusations that she knew nothing of her husband's murder. He scolds her for marrying Claudius. The ghost appears, but Gertrude cannot see it. When Hamlet talks to it, she is certain he is mad. He tells her he is only pretending to be mad, but she must not let the king know that. He then leaves, taking Polonius's corpse with him.

Lesson 25: The Two Adversaries and Their Allies

Lesson 2 suggests that *Hamlet* can be seen as a contest between two powerful enemies, Hamlet and Claudius. It is in Act III that their contest really begins, for then Hamlet gets the proof that his father's murderer is Claudius. As for Claudius, he realizes that Hamlet is a threat to him, one that he must get rid of.

Claudius's position assures him of allies, courtiers willing to lower themselves to gain the king's favor. Hamlet, on the other hand, can trust only Horatio. He tells Horatio his suspicions and asks Horatio's help in watching Claudius during the play. By the end of Act III, however, Gertrude's loyalty is to her son, and Hamlet trusts her enough to confess that his madness is not real.

The following questions will further your understanding of the two major characters and their respective allies.

1. Until Claudius perceives Hamlet as an enemy (in this act), what tells you that he is trying to treat Hamlet kindly? Why does he want to win Hamlet over?

_____

2. Shakespeare portrays Claudius as an overly ambitious man. Is he totally without conscience? Make references to the play to prove your point.

_____

3. In his speech to Polonius after they have spied on Hamlet and Ophelia, how does Claudius show that he is a man of keen perceptions?

_____

4. Why is it so important to Hamlet at this time that his friend Horatio is quite unexcitable and of sound judgment?

_____

5. Why is Gertrude able to watch the play without becoming emotionally involved in it? (*Clue:* Think about her reaction later that night to Hamlet's accusation of murder.)

_____

6. When Hamlet compares himself to the recorder that Guildenstern says he cannot play, how is Hamlet scolding Guildenstern? How does that rebuke show that he, like Claudius, is a man of keen perception?

_____

7. In his soliloquy at the end of Act III, Scene II, lines 406–417, does Hamlet show that he does not entirely trust his self-control?

_____

8. Why are Rosencrantz and Guildenstern willing to betray their friendship with Hamlet and do as Claudius asks? Is their motivation the same as Polonius's when he stoops to spying on Hamlet and Ophelia or Hamlet and his mother?

_____

9. Hamlet thinks before he acts. Why can't he bring himself to kill Claudius, presumably at his prayers? To Hamlet, how is Claudius's state different from King Hamlet's when Claudius killed him?

_____

10. Why does Hamlet seem so callous about having murdered Polonius?

_____

11. At the end of this act, how has Hamlet's opinion of his mother changed?

_____

12. Hamlet shows his perceptiveness again in his comments about his erstwhile friends, Rosencrantz and Guildenstern. How does he now regard them?

_____

Reading Quiz: *Hamlet,* Act III

1. What indication is there that Gertrude would be happy to see Hamlet and Ophelia marry?

   _____

   _____

2. In his conversation with Ophelia, while Claudius and Polonius listen in, where does Hamlet tell her she should go?

   _____

   _____

3. Stated briefly, what is Hamlet's main instruction to the players about how they should perform?

   _____

   _____

4. What is Gertrude's reaction to the player-queen?

   _____

   _____

5. When Rosencrantz questions Hamlet again about the cause of his "distemper," what does Hamlet say is bothering him?

   _____

   _____

6. What is Hamlet's reaction when he realizes he has killed Polonius?

   _____

   _____

What Happens in Act IV, *Hamlet*

Act IV, Scene I Gertrude tells Claudius that Hamlet, in his madness, has killed Polonius. Claudius realizes that Hamlet is sane and probably intended the sword thrust for him. But he says to Gertrude that because Hamlet is mad, he is a threat to all of them. He tells her that the public will be critical that Hamlet was not restrained before this. He plans to send Hamlet to England immediately and will inform his counselors of the murder and his plans for Hamlet's departure. Thus he hopes to avoid a scandal that might weaken his own position. He sends Rosencrantz and Guildenstern to find Polonius's body and take it to the chapel.

Act IV, Scene II Rosencrantz and Guildenstern approach Hamlet, asking where Polonius's body is. He is flippant with them and still pretends to be mad. He tells them, in effect, that the king is using them and will discard them when he is through.

Act IV, Scene III Alone, Claudius voices his thoughts. He must be careful in his treatment of Hamlet because the people love him and would resent his being punished. Rosencrantz reports that Polonius's body has not been found. Then Guildenstern brings in Hamlet. When the king asks Hamlet where he has put Polonius's corpse, Hamlet says it is food for the worms. Claudius is outwardly patient with Hamlet and tells him that, for his own safety, he must leave for England immediately. After Hamlet goes out, the king instructs Rosencrantz and Guildenstern to get Hamlet aboard ship at once; it is to sail that night. Alone again, Claudius reveals in a soliloquy that he has sent letters to the king of England, asking that Hamlet be put to death. The king is under obligation to Claudius and will do what he wants.

Act IV, Scene IV Fortinbras and his troops are marching across Denmark to Poland. Hamlet meets one of the officers and finds that these Norwegians are going to risk their lives for a bit of worthless land. He then scolds himself that with so many good reasons to act, he himself has taken no revenge.

Act IV, Scene V Gertrude has been told that Ophelia is talking nonsense and that her words are making people suspicious about Polonius's death. She agrees to see the girl. Ophelia comes in singing snatches of song mixed in with a few words that make sense. She is unaware of her surroundings. Claudius, realizing Ophelia's mental state, asks Horatio to follow her and watch out for her. Claudius then recites to Gertrude all the woes that have befallen their kingdom— Polonius's death, Hamlet's hasty departure, and Ophelia's madness. Laertes has returned to Denmark, convinced that Claudius is responsible for his father's death. After a commotion outside the door, Laertes comes in. He addresses Claudius as "vile king" and vows revenge. While Claudius tries to calm him and assures him that he had no part in Polonius's death, Ophelia comes in. Laertes realizes that she is mad. Claudius sympathizes with him for his two sorrows, says again that he had nothing to do with Polonius's death, and promises him revenge on the guilty one.

Act IV, Scene VI Horatio receives a letter from Hamlet in which he describes a pirate attack on his ship and being captured. He tells Horatio that the pirates have brought him back to Denmark and asks Horatio to come to him.

Act IV, Scene VII Claudius has convinced Laertes that Hamlet killed Polonius and intended to kill Claudius himself. A note arrives from Hamlet, announcing his return. Laertes wants to take immediate revenge, but Claudius says there is a way he can have his revenge yet make Hamlet's death seem accidental. Claudius's scheme involves a fencing match with Hamlet, for which Laertes will use an unblunted sword with a poisoned tip. Gertrude comes in with the sad news that Ophelia has drowned. Laertes leaves, grief-stricken.

Lesson 26: Discovering Contrasts Between Characters and Within the Characters Themselves

In Act III, just as Hamlet finds proof of Claudius's guilt, Claudius learns that Hamlet's madness is not real and that Hamlet is probably a threat to him. Claudius takes immediate action to banish Hamlet and have him killed. But Hamlet still has not taken his revenge. Thus Shakespeare sets up a contrast between Claudius, the man of action, and Hamlet, the man of thought.

In Act IV, the actions of Fortinbras and Laertes are in contrast to Hamlet's inaction. Hamlet himself notes that Fortinbras is leading his troops against the Poles, apparently without considering whether the prize is worth the risk. As for Laertes, he returns from France intent on revenge for his father's death. He is ready to challenge his king

without being certain whether or not Claudius is guilty. Just as readily, he falls in with Claudius's scheme to kill Hamlet by a trick that Hamlet, the man of honor, will not suspect.

But also in Act IV, Hamlet acts impulsively when he kills Polonius, and apparently he is not very remorseful. Also, in his disillusionment, he is cruel to both Ophelia and Gertrude. Even the hero, then, has his faults, for it is part of Shakespeare's genius that he creates not black or white characters but believable human beings with both faults and virtues.

Answering the following questions will make you more aware of the many sides of Shakespeare's characters.

1. Reread the opening dialogue between Claudius and Gertrude in Act IV, Scene I. How accurately is Gertrude describing how Hamlet killed Polonius? How much of her interview with Hamlet does she reveal to Claudius?

2. Do you think Gertrude's attitude toward Claudius has changed? Explain.

3. Now look at Act IV, Scene V, beginning with line 112, as Laertes bursts in upon Claudius and Gertrude. How would you describe Gertrude's attitude toward Laertes? How does it reflect her attitude toward her husband?

4. At the beginning of Scene V, why is Gertrude reluctant to see Ophelia? (*Clue:* See her speech in lines 16–20.)

5. Why are Ophelia's snatches of bawdy songs both startling and sad?

6. Is Claudius sincerely sorry about Polonius's death and Ophelia's mental state? On what do you base your opinion?

7. Claudius gives Laertes two reasons for not having taken action against Hamlet sooner (Scene VII, lines 9–24). Is he honest in both cases? Explain.

8. What is particularly unpleasant about the way Claudius and Laertes plan to kill Hamlet? (*Clue:* Remember that both must have been educated as gentlemen and taught a code of honor.)

9. Reread Laertes's speech in Scene VII, lines 186–192. How does it reveal both the best and the worst in his nature?

Reading Quiz: *Hamlet,* **Act IV**

1. Hamlet finally tells the king where he has hidden Polonius's body. Where is it?

   _____

   _____

2. When a messenger says that Ophelia would like to see the queen, who advises Gertrude to see her?

   _____

   _____

3. What is the mood of Laertes' followers just before he confronts Claudius?

   _____

   _____

4. What skill of Laertes did the Norman, Lamound, talk about and praise in Claudius's court?

   _____

   _____

5. From Gertrude's description, what caused Ophelia's drowning?

   _____

   _____

6. When Laertes leaves after hearing of his sister's death, what lie does Claudius tell Gertrude about his conversation with Laertes?

   _____

   _____

What Happens in Act V, *Hamlet*

Act V, Scene I While they are digging a grave for a gentlewoman, the sexton (church employee or officer) and his helper argue about whether or not she should have a Christian burial since she drowned herself. Hamlet and Horatio approach, unnoticed, as the gravedigger tosses out a skull he has just uncovered. Hamlet says that it may have been the skull of someone who held an important position. Now its owner is no more, and the skull is tossed rudely aside.

Hamlet asks the sexton whose grave he is preparing. The man does not answer directly, but does identify the skull as Yorick's. Yorick was the court jester whom Hamlet, as a child, knew and loved. Now only his bones remain. Hamlet points

out to Horatio that thus all people eventually return to dust and obscurity.

Hamlet and Horatio see a funeral procession approaching. In it are the king, the queen, and members of the court. Out of sight of the mourners, Hamlet and Horatio watch. Hamlet recognizes Laertes and soon realizes that it is Ophelia's funeral. When Laertes, overcome with grief, leaps into the grave, Hamlet comes forward and leaps in, too. Laertes attacks Hamlet, who defends himself. Hamlet assumes that Laertes attacked because he was determined to show his great grief for his sister. Hamlet then says that his love for Ophelia was greater than any brother's. Gertrude and Claudius beg Laertes to restrain himself since Hamlet is obviously mad.

Hamlet and the gravedigger

(continued)

What Happens in Act V, *Hamlet* (continued)

Act V, Scene II Hamlet describes to Horatio how, aboard ship, he stole the packet of letters Rosencrantz and Guildenstern were delivering to the king of England. Hamlet read them and discovered that Claudius was asking the king to have him beheaded. Hamlet substituted some letters he wrote himself, asking that the bearers (Rosencrantz and Guildenstern) be put to death immediately. Next day, the sea fight occurred, and he returned to Denmark with the pirates. Horatio agrees that Hamlet must take his revenge quickly before Claudius learns about this.

A member of the court, Osric, comes in to tell Hamlet that Claudius has set up a fencing contest and a bet, pitting Hamlet against Laertes, if Hamlet will agree. Hamlet does, but tells Horatio that he has misgivings about the match. Horatio urges him not to go through with it, but Hamlet pays him no mind.

Before the match, Hamlet asks Laertes' pardon if, in his madness, he has wronged him. Laertes answers in a hypocritical way, seeming to accept Hamlet's explanation of his behavior. Falsely, Claudius seems to be Hamlet's champion, saying that cannon fire, drums, and trumpets will mark Hamlet's success. He then "drinks to Hamlet." Hamlet is now winning, and Claudius urges him to drink too, but Hamlet is not ready. Instead, Gertrude drinks from the poisoned cup that Claudius had intended for Hamlet. Laertes wounds Hamlet with the unblunted sword. They scuffle and exchange swords. Hamlet now has the sword with the poisoned tip, and he wounds Laertes. The king tries to stop the match. Gertrude collapses. Both contestants are bleeding. Laertes realizes that his own trickery will now be the cause of his death. Dying, Gertrude calls out to Hamlet that the drink is poisoned. Laertes now collapses, but confesses to Hamlet about the poisoned sword, blaming Claudius. Hamlet wounds Claudius and gives him the poisoned wine. Claudius dies. Just before Laertes dies, he asks Hamlet to exchange forgiveness with him. Hamlet is dying. Horatio is about to commit suicide, but Hamlet says he must live to tell Hamlet's story and clear his name.

Fortinbras arrives, victorious, and Hamlet, dying, predicts Fortinbras will be Denmark's new king. Fortinbras accepts the authority, gives a tribute to Hamlet, and says that he will have a hero's burial.

Lesson 27: A Close Look at the Final Act

The Elizabethans of Shakespeare's original audience were familiar with the so-called revenge tragedy in which a father takes revenge for his son or a son for his father. The ghost of the murder victim, the scheming villain, real or pretended insanity, and multiple murders were all part of such plays. *Hamlet* thus certainly qualifies as a play of murder and revenge. But it is a complicated play and can be interpreted several ways.

What is more, Hamlet and Claudius are not your typical hero and villain. Consider the following:

Hamlet, the tragic hero, is honor-bound to take revenge for his father's murder, but he finds it difficult to do:

The time is out of joint, O cursed spite
That ever I was born to set it right!

Claudius, the "scheming villain," is overcome with remorse:

O, my offence is rank, it smells to heaven;
It has the primal eldest curse upon't,
A brother's murder!

Hamlet, the hero, is responsible for the deaths of Polonius, Rosencrantz, and Guildenstern. Claudius, the villain, tries to pray and longs for God's forgiveness. (He is still capable of cold-bloodedly ordering Hamlet's death and later of maneuvering Laertes into murdering Hamlet.) In short, hero and villain, unlike the characters in the typical revenge plays, are so complex that both have had a variety of interpretations on the stage.

Like today's audience, Shakespeare's audience would have expected some kind of solution (called the **dénouement**) in the final act of the tragedy, and in Act V, it does occur. Hamlet's actions are justified, he has his revenge, and the king's villainy is exposed.

Now let's look at some interesting sidelights in the final act. Answers to the following questions will emphasize these sidelights.

1. The gravediggers' task is a sobering one, but their conversation is humorous. Why do you suppose Shakespeare creates humor at this time? Assuming that the play mirrors real life, why might the men joke at such a time?

_____

2. What general view of life does Hamlet express in his comments to Horatio in the graveyard?

_____

3. Why does the priest insist that the burial service for Ophelia be brief?

_____

4. How would you describe the courtier Osric? Does he remind you of someone else in the play? Explain.

_____

5. Throughout the play, it is clear that Claudius loves Gertrude dearly. Yet in this act, he tells her not to drink the wine but does not tell her it is poisoned. How do you account for that?

_____

6. What final compliment does Fortinbras, the man of action, give to Hamlet?

_____

Reading Quiz: *Hamlet,* Act V

1. According to the second gravedigger, why is Ophelia, who committed suicide, being given a Christian burial?

   _____

   _____

2. What characterizes the gravedigger's answers when Hamlet questions him?

   _____

   _____

3. In the graveyard, as Queen Gertrude is scattering flowers on Ophelia's grave, what does she say that she once hoped would happen?

   _____

   _____

4. What is Hamlet and Horatio's attitude toward Osric?

   _____

   _____

5. When does the audience find out what finally happened to Rosencrantz and Guildenstern?

   _____

   _____

6. To what event is Hamlet referring in his speech before the fencing match?

   > *If it be now, 'tis not to come; if it be not to come, it will*
   > *be now; if it be not now, yet it will come: the readiness is all.*
   > *Since no man knows aught of what he leaves, what is 't to leave betimes?*

   _____

   _____

7. Why does Hamlet, dying, take the trouble to name a successor to the throne of Denmark?

   _____

   _____

Lesson 28: Glimpses of Shakespeare's World in *Hamlet*

The setting of a play is the place and time of the action. All of the action in *Hamlet* takes place in or near the castle of Elsinore in Denmark. The total time elapsed in the play is between two and three months.

A broader definition of setting would involve more than just those details, for you, the reader, are also learning something about the daily life of the characters and about their religious and moral attitudes. Of course, *Hamlet* is based on a historical account of a Danish prince who lived sometime before the tenth century, but the characters in the play behave like sixteenth-century English people. Thus, Shakespeare's setting gives you glimpses of his world—England in the time of Elizabeth I.

In finding the answers to the following questions, you will be learning a little social history.

1. King James, I, Queen Elizabeth's successor, was the author of a book called *Daemonologie* (Demonology), in which he wrote of his fear of the spirit world. In Act I of *Hamlet,* what indications are there that even university-educated people were superstitious and believed in ghosts?

_____

_____

2. In his speech to Hamlet in Act I, Scene V, lines 9–20, the ghost is evidently describing purgatory. In lines 76–79, he describes the circumstances of his death. Why would Shakespeare's audience have expected King Hamlet's spirit to be doomed to spend time in purgatory?

_____

_____

3. Laertes tells his sister how to behave, and Polonius forbids her to have any conversation with Hamlet. She tells her father that she will obey. If Ophelia is typical of well-brought-up young women of her time, what would you suspect their position in the family was?

_____

_____

4. Both Hamlet and his father see Gertrude's marriage to Claudius as incestuous, yet it would not be regarded so today. What prohibition of that period do you infer from Hamlet and his father's attitude?

_____

_____

5. Shakespeare, a monarchist, believed that to depose or kill the rightful monarch would bring chaos to the kingdom. How is this belief brought out in the ghost's speech in Act I, Scene V, lines 35–40? Can you see why Hamlet names a successor to the Danish throne? Explain.

_____

_____

(continued)

Lesson 28:
Glimpses of Shakespeare's World in *Hamlet* (continued)

6. Act II, Scene II, lines 339–360, contain one of the few topical references in Shakespeare's plays. What problem faced by the actors of his period is Shakespeare describing? (*Clue:* Your footnotes should help you here.)

    _____

    _____

7. The gravediggers' discussion and the priest's remarks give you a clue as to the Elizabethan attitude toward suicide. What was it?

    _____

    _____

8. Claudius's apparent reason for banishing Hamlet was to rid the kingdom of a madman. In fact, he is afraid people will think he should have done it earlier. What do you infer was the commonly held attitude toward mental illness?

    _____

    _____

9. At the opening of Act III, Scene II, Hamlet gives lengthy instructions to the actors. From the things he warns them not to do, what do you infer might have been typical stage behavior of the time? What kind of behavior did Hamlet (Shakespeare) prefer?

    _____

    _____

10. When Laertes comes in threatening, Claudius is calm, saying,

    There's such divinity doth hedge a king
    That treason can but peep to what it would   (Can only look, not act)

    What well-known belief about monarchs is Claudius describing?

    _____

    _____

Lesson 29: Shakespeare's Language

As you have learned, Hamlet is based on the life of a Danish prince who lived hundreds of years before Shakespeare, and Shakespeare was not the first to retell the prince's story. Some audiences may have been familiar with a previous Hamlet play. They may have known in advance how Shakespeare's would end, but they were eager to hear the language he would use to tell the story.

Elizabethans (sometimes described as "a nest of singing birds") were in love with language and song. A gentleman needed to sing and play a musical instrument to serenade his lady, and he probably needed to write fairly good poetry, assuring her of his eternal devotion. People were fond of puns and delighted in lively conversation, such as the exchange between Hamlet and the gravedigger.

To be able to embroider conversation with clever plays on words, elaborate metaphors, or newly made up words was an important social grace, especially in Queen Elizabeth's court. But no one else used the language with such great skill as William Shakespeare.

Catering to the Elizabethan fondness for music, Shakespeare included songs in many plays, but he did not simply add music for its own sake. His songs fitted into the story. An example is Ophelia's song, a sad lament for her father, in Act IV, Scene V, lines 29–32, 35, and 37–39. Her other snatches of song, about a faithless lover, echo her father and brother's warnings to her about Hamlet.

Let's look at other scenes in *Hamlet* where Shakespeare's language shows this style.

1. In Act II, Scene II, lines 116–124, Polonius reads aloud Hamlet's letter to Ophelia. In what ways is it a typical English gentleman's love letter?

_____

2. In his first speech in the play, Act I, Scene II, line 65, Hamlet says in an aside, "A little more than kin, and less than kind!" Hamlet is saying that now, as Claudius's stepson, he is a little more than kin to him. (*Kin* referred to relatives outside the immediate family.) In "less than kind," Hamlet puns, for although *kind* meant son, and he is now Claudius's son, Hamlet uses the word to mean that his feelings toward Claudius are not kind. To test your understanding of puns, try another speech—Act V, Scene I, Hamlet's reply to the clown, lines 136–138. How does Hamlet's use of the word *lie* pun on the clown's use of the same word in the previous speech?

_____

3. A metaphor is an implied comparison, one that we use often in ordinary speech. When we talk, for example, about the eye of a needle, a head of lettuce, or the body of an essay, we compare a part of the human body to each object. Let's look at a Shakespearean metaphor, the opening of his famous Sonnet LXXIII:

> That time of year thou mayst in me behold
> When yellow leaves, or none, or few, do hang
> Upon those boughs which shake against the cold
> Bare ruined choirs where late the sweet birds sang.

His message is that he is growing old, but he doesn't say that directly; he uses a metaphor, comparing himself to an almost leafless tree in the late autumn cold. Now read Claudius's comment to Laertes in Act IV, Scene VII, lines 111–118. What is he saying metaphorically about love and time?

_____

4. Define as many as possible of the following words.

obscene _____   dislocate _____

hot-blooded _____   heartsick _____

assassination _____   premeditated _____

barefaced _____   invulnerable _____

Could you define most of them? All are in common use today and are among the more than 1,700 that appeared *first* in Shakespeare's plays. They are words he apparently made up himself!

Lesson 30: Shakespeare's Poetry

You may already know that Shakespeare's plays are written in blank verse and that, although he was not the first to use it, no one used blank verse more skilfully. Let's take time to review what **blank verse** is. Briefly defined, it is **unrhymed iambic pentameter**. Let's break that definition down a bit.

An *iamb* is a poetic measure called a **foot**. It is made up of two syllables, with the accent on the second. The word *today* is a perfect iamb. *Penta,* from the Greek, means five, and *meter* refers to the rhythmic pattern of a poem (in this case, a five-measure line). Putting it all together, an iambic

pentameter line has five feet, each foot (iamb) having two syllables, with the accent or beat on the second. It might be diagrammed like this:

Today/ Today/ Today/ Today/ Today/
  1   2   3   4   5

Now look at one of Shakespeare's iambic pentameter lines in Act I, Scene IV, line 8 of *Hamlet.*

The king/ doth wake/ tonight/ and takes/ his rouse.
   1   2   3   4   5

1. Divide the following line into five iambic feet and mark the accented syllables.

   I stay too long. But here my father comes.

Shakespeare sometimes rhymed his iambic pentameter lines, particularly at the end of a scene. For example, in Act II, Scene II, the closing lines of Hamlet's speech are:

   More relative than this. The play's the thing
   Wherein I'll catch the conscience of the king.

   (Can you divide these two lines into iambic pentameter?)

One theory is that Shakespeare used rhyme to close a scene because actors waiting to go on could learn, or hear, a rhymed line more easily and would be ready to make their appearance on stage on cue.

As you read *Hamlet,* you may have noted that not every line of the play is in blank verse or even in poetry. Particularly when ordinary people such as the gravediggers are talking, the speeches are in prose. But it is not always the artisans, or "rude mechanicals" as they were called in Shakespeare's day, that speak in prose. One of Hamlet's most famous speeches, beginning in line 304 of Act II, Scene II, is in prose also. Let's look carefully now at lines 314–323 of that speech, in which Shakespeare gives a tribute to mankind. What devices does he use to make those lines so impressive? First of all, notice his words; each is so well chosen that he needs only a few to get his point across.

2. Define the following words from that speech. (Use a dictionary if necessary.)

   infinite _____ express _____

   faculties _____ paragon _____

   apprehension _____

3. Now list all the metaphors and similes you can find in those lines. Remember that both are comparisons, but a simile uses *like* or *as.* (For example, "you are as welcome as the flowers in May.")

   _____

Note too that part of Shakespeare's effect is gained by repeating grammatical structure, as in "how noble in reason!" "how infinite in faculties!" Such deliberate repetition impresses the words upon the reader's or hearer's mind. It is called **parallel structure**.

4. Any examination of Shakespeare's poetry makes you aware of his skillful use of adjectives to achieve his wonderful word pictures. Reread Gertrude's description of Ophelia's death in Act IV, Scene VII, lines 168–184. Now, in one sentence, using no adjectives, state how Ophelia died.

   _____

Do you see how dull the factual statement is when compared with Gertrude's lines?

Name _____ Date _____

Final Test: *Hamlet*

Complete the following statements in the fewest possible words.

1. Claudius sends Cornelius and Voltimand to Norway to _____.

2. Hamlet's anger is directed toward his mother because _____.

3. Polonius and Laertes warn Ophelia against Hamlet because _____.

4. The ghost appears to Hamlet to ask him to _____.

5. Hamlet decides to play the madman in order to _____.

6. Polonius sends Reynaldo to France to _____.

7. Claudius summons Rosencrantz and Guildenstern to court to _____.

8. Hamlet decides to set a trap for Claudius by _____.

9. Claudius realizes that he cannot pray for forgiveness because _____.

10. Polonius's meddling causes his _____.

11. Claudius sends Hamlet to England, intending to have him _____ there;
    instead, Rosencrantz and Guildenstern _____ there.

12. Ophelia's madness is caused by _____, _____, and _____.

13. The priest's burial service for Ophelia is very brief because _____.

14. Laertes's evil scheming with Claudius results in his own _____.

Who is the speaker in each extract below?

15. *The time is out of joint: O cursed spite,*
    That ever I was born to set it right!   _____

16. *Get thee to a nunnery;*   _____

17. *O, my offence is rank, it smells to heaven;*
    It hath the primal eldest curse upon 't,   _____

18. *O Hamlet, speak no more;*
    Thou turn'st mine eyes into my very soul;
    And there I see such black and grained spots   _____

19. *I will speak daggers to her, but use none;*   _____

20. *For he was likely, had he been put on,*
    To have proved most royal: and, for his passage,
    The soldiers' music and the rites of war   _____

21. You have learned that one theme in *Hamlet* is the difficulty people face in distinguishing between reality (what is) and illusion (what seems to be). **Show how any one of the following illustrates that theme.** Write your answer on the back of this paper.

    A. Hamlet's misgivings about the ghost

    B. Ophelia's misunderstanding of Hamlet's behavior once he has seen the ghost

    C. Gertrude's lack of knowledge of Claudius's character

    D. Laertes' willingness to accept Claudius's explanation of Polonius's death

To the Teacher:

Suggestions for Presenting *A Midsummer Night's Dream*

Sources

Students may be interested to know that Shakespeare's sources for this play were probably actual events at the court of Queen Elizabeth I. At least two weddings (that of Elizabeth Vere to the earl of Derby and that of Thomas, son of Lord Berkely, to Elizabeth, daughter of Sir George Carey) may have been the inspiration for Theseus's wedding celebration. Another occasion that may have inspired some of the play's descriptions was an entertainment in Elizabeth's honor, arranged by her favorite courtier, Leicester. Titania has been identified as Queen Elizabeth herself, and Oberon is said to represent Henry VIII (Elizabeth's father). The changeling boy, some scholars believe, was the son of Lady Catherine Grey, a boy who was supposed to have some claim to the throne of England. Thus, this play is more closely related to events at court than are most of Shakespeare's others.

Topics for Class Discussion

Ask several volunteers to research arranged marriages, which were common in Europe until recent times. Students might want to consult a social history or encyclopedia for information on this topic. Remind them that an arranged marriage is part of the plot of both *Romeo and Juliet* and the modern musical *Fiddler on the Roof*. Point out that marriages of European royalty were often arranged. Have the students report to the class, using the reports as a basis for a class discussion about whether or not arranged marriages are a good idea.

Topics for Oral Reports

Remind students that Shakespeare grew up in the same small village to which he retired after spending his working life in London. The flowers he mentions in the plays are the ones he would have known from the meadows of Stratford. Ask a student or students to find out what they can about each of these flowers: thyme, violet, musk-rose, eglantine, and love-in-idleness, including their medicinal properties, if any; beliefs and superstitions about these flowers; and their significance in the language of flowers. Two possible sources are *Shakespeare's Flowers* by Jessica Kerr and *Culpepper's Complete Herbal*. Ask students to share their information with the class.

One or more students could consult William Butler Yeats's *Fairy and Folk Tales of Ireland* or similar sources to discover what characteristics various fairies, such as the fairy shoemaker (otherwise known as the leprechaun), were supposed to possess. Again, have the students report to the class.

Hands-on Activities

For students who like to sketch, suggest making poster-size drawings of Oberon, Titania, and Puck. They could use pastel crayons to color the drawings and then hang them on the bulletin board.

For students who like to perform, a class presentation of *Pyramus and Thisby* is a worthwhile project. Ask them to use Shakespeare's dialogue and to improvise costumes, just as the artisans did.

A Student-Produced Review

This exercise includes all students and provides a thorough review of the details of the play. Assign each student about a half-page in the play, on which he or she will base one factual question. (It could even be a question about a footnoted vocabulary word.) Then divide the class into two teams. Each student should ask a question of the member of the opposite team whose turn it is. If that person's answer is correct, the team gets two points. If he or she cannot answer, but another team member can, the team gets one point. If no one on that team can answer, one point goes to the team asking the question. Play continues until all students' questions have been asked.

What Happens in Act I, *A Midsummer Night's Dream*

Act I, Scene I In four days, Theseus, Duke of Athens, is to marry Hippolyta, queen of the Amazons (a race of female warriors). He tells his bride-to-be that although he has wooed her with his sword (conquered her), he will wed her with great ceremony and celebration. He sends his attendant, Philostrate, into the streets to urge everyone to make merry.

Egeus arrives with his daughter Hermia and her two suitors, Demetrius and Lysander. He complains to the duke that Hermia refuses to marry Demetrius. Instead, she wants to marry Lysander, who, according to Egeus, has stolen her affections. He claims his right under the law to put her to death if she continues to disobey him by refusing to marry the man he has chosen for her.

The duke tries to persuade Hermia to marry Demetrius. If she will not, she must either become a nun or be killed. She must make up her mind by the day of his wedding.

Hermia's father and the suitors begin to argue. Finally, Lysander accuses Demetrius of leading on another woman, Helena, and then dropping her. The duke remarks that he has already heard this rumor about Demetrius. He and Hippolyta then leave, taking Demetrius and Egeus with them.

The lovers, left alone, at first bemoan their fate. Then Lysander offers a plan. They will meet the following night at his aunt's house seven leagues out of Athens. (A league is about three miles.) Thus they will be outside Athens' jurisdiction and will be free to marry.

At that point, Hermia's friend Helena comes in, sorrowing that Demetrius no longer loves her and wants to marry Hermia. Hermia protests that she has done nothing to encourage him. She and Lysander tell Helena that they plan to marry secretly the following night. After they leave, Helena decides to tell Demetrius of the lovers' plan, hoping that by doing so, she will improve her own chances with him.

Act I, Scene II A group of artisans are gathered at the home of Peter Quince, a carpenter. They are choosing parts for a play they will perform to entertain Duke Theseus and his bride. It is to be "The Most Cruel Death of Pyramus and Thisby," hardly the choice for a wedding feast, but the artisans are enthusiastic about performing it. Bottom, the weaver, is assigned the lover's part, Pyramus. Actually, Bottom is eager to take every part mentioned. Flute, the bellows mender (a bellows is a device whose sides are squeezed to push air into something), is to be Thisby. He protests playing a woman's part because he has "a beard coming." The tailor and the tinker (a person who travels from place to place mending things) are assigned minor parts, and Snug, the joiner (who makes wooden furniture and house fittings) is to play the lion. He worries about memorizing his lines! After all the parts are distributed, Quince tells his players to learn their parts and meet him the following night in the palace wood, where they can rehearse.

         The Complete Guide to Shakespeare's Best Plays

Name _____ Date _____

Lesson 31: Identifying the Plots of *A Midsummer Night's Dream*

You already know that the plot of a novel or play is actually the story—in other words, "what happens next." In this play, Shakespeare has constructed four parallel plots. First is the love story of Duke Theseus and his bride-to-be. As the chief judge, Theseus is also involved in the lives of his subjects and therefore in the other plots.

Next come the accounts of (2) Demetrius, who loves Hermia; (3) Hermia, who loves Lysander; and (4) Helena, who loves Demetrius. How will these lovers' problems be solved so that everyone is happy in the end?

You probably are interested in the earnest artisans, too. Will they succeed in their well-meaning but bungling attempt to present a play to the duke? Will they become more involved in the others' lives and problems?

Finally, another plot will unfold. You have yet to meet the principal characters in that plot, but you may be certain that this play has enough action to hold your attention as it did that of Shakespeare's audience when it was first performed four hundred years ago.

To be certain that you have a clear understanding of the plots so far, try answering the following questions. If necessary, refer back to the play.

1. As the play opens, what is making Theseus slightly impatient? How does Hippolyta calm him?

   _____

   _____

2. With the arrival of Egeus, his daughter, and her suitors, what problem becomes apparent—a problem about which the duke, as magistrate, will be expected to make a judgment?

   _____

   _____

3. What indication is there that Demetrius, the man Egeus wants his daughter to marry, may not be the ideal choice?

   _____

   _____

4. What plan does Lysander suggest to Hermia as a way out of their difficulties?

   _____

   _____

5. Do you think Helena is jealous of Hermia's beauty? Explain. _____

   _____

6. Without knowing any details of the play the artisans will perform, what does Quince say about it that suggests it may not be appropriate as a performance on the duke's wedding day?

   _____

   _____

Reading Quiz: *A Midsummer Night's Dream,* **Act I**

1. The people of Shakespeare's day looked for omens in the weather. In fact, we still say, "Happy the bride the sun shines on." What good omen will be seen for the wedding of Theseus and Hippolyta?

   _____

   _____

2. What will be the consequences if Hermia continues to refuse Demetrius, thus disobeying her father?

   _____

   _____

3. What evidence does Lysander give that Demetrius is inconstant in love?

   _____

   _____

4. By telling Demetrius what Lysander and Hermia told her in confidence, what does Helena hope to regain?

   _____

   _____

5. Among the artisans, which one seems most confident of his acting ability?

   _____

(continued)

What Happens in Act II, *A Midsummer Night's Dream*

Act II, Scene I It is night in a forest near Athens. Puck (Robin Goodfellow) meets a fairy and asks where she is going. She says she is preparing for the arrival of the fairy queen, Titania. Puck tells her that the fairy king, Oberon, is quarreling with his Titania because she has stolen a little mortal boy, who is now her page. Jealous Oberon wants the child in his own troop.

Oberon and Titania, with their followers, arrive from opposite directions and immediately begin to quarrel. Titania accuses him of loving Hippolyta, who is about to wed Duke Theseus. Oberon accuses her of being overly fond of Theseus and causing him to be unfaithful in his relationships with women. She then points out that their own quarreling is causing all kinds of trouble to mortals. He counters that they need quarrel no more if she will give him the little boy. She refuses. The child's mother, who was her friend, died in childbirth, and Titania has vowed to take care of the boy.

Apparently trying to make peace, Titania invites Oberon to join her and her attendants in their dancing. He won't unless she gives him the boy. She refuses again and leaves to avoid further quarrels.

Still annoyed, Oberon vows revenge. To that end, he sends Puck to find a little flower, love-in-idleness, whose juice, he says, is so potent that sprinkled on the eyelids of a sleeping person, it will make that person fall madly in love with the first creature he or she sees upon awakening.

Alone, Oberon thinks aloud in a soliloquy (a speech given while the actor is alone on the stage). He says that he will put the flower juice on Titania's eyelids while she is sleeping. Then she will wake up and fall in love with whoever first appears. He vows that he will not remove the spell until she allows him to have the mortal child.

Oberon then makes himself invisible as Demetrius appears, with Helena following. He is telling her to leave him alone, for he does not love her. He is searching for Hermia and Lysander. Driven by his love for Hermia, he intends to kill his rival. Helena refuses to leave. Again, Demetrius says he does not love her and does nothing to encourage her. She says she is like a faithful spaniel who will not be driven away. He scolds her for being immodest and threatens to leave her at the mercy of the wild beasts. Nothing discourages her. When he leaves, she still follows.

Having heard their conversation, Oberon vows that before Demetrius and Helena leave the forest, Demetrius will be pursuing her, and she will be fleeing from him.

Puck returns with the remarkable flower juice. Oberon tells Puck that he knows where Titania is sleeping. He will go there and put some on her eyelids. He tells Puck to take some juice and put it on the eyelids of "a disdainful youth" (Demetrius) so that he will fall in love with a sweet Athenian lady (Helena). Thus Oberon hopes to make Helena happy by helping her regain Demetrius's love. Puck goes to do as Oberon says.

Act II, Scene II Titania appears with her attendants and assigns them some tasks, one being to sing her to sleep. She sleeps, and the fairies depart, leaving only one to guard her. Oberon appears, sprinkles the flower juice on Titania's eyelids, recites a magic chant, and leaves.

Lysander and Hermia appear. She is weary, and Lysander has lost the way. They decide to lie down to rest. Modestly, Hermia tells Lysander to lie at some distance from her. He does, and they sleep. Puck comes in, and mistaking Lysander for Demetrius, sprinkles his eyelids with the potion so that he will wake up and love the first creature he sees.

(continued)

What Happens in Act II, *A Midsummer Night's Dream* (continued)

Demetrius and Helena arrive. She is still pleading with him to stay with her, but he leaves almost immediately. Alone, Helena compares herself with Hermia. She thinks Hermia has all the beauty and that this is why Demetrius prefers her.

Suddenly, she sees Lysander asleep or dead on the ground and tries to wake him. He wakes and immediately loves Helena, asking where Demetrius is so that he can kill him. Helena tells him not to talk that way about Demetrius, even though he is in love with Lysander's Hermia. Lysander rejects the thought of Hermia, saying that he was too young and lacked reason, but that now he recognizes that Helena is far superior to Hermia. Helena thinks he is merely pretending affection. Knowing that she is despised by one man and thinking that she is being mocked by another, she leaves, unhappy.

Alone, Lysander looks at Hermia, who is still asleep. He tells himself that he now hates her and will do everything in his power to love and honor Helena. He leaves Hermia alone in the forest. She awakes from a bad dream and cries out for him. Realizing that she is alone, she vows to find her beloved Lysander or die in the attempt.

Puck and the fairies

Name _____ Date _____

Lesson 32: Fairies, Mortals, and Mistaken Identities

In Act II, Shakespeare introduces yet another plot, this one involving supernatural beings whose moods and actions affect mortals. His original audience would have had no difficulty accepting a play that blended reality with fantasy. People believed in fairies, just as they believed in witches and demons. In fact, they employed a variety of charms to ward off evil spirits of all kinds.

Shakespeare is careful to set the stage, though. The action takes place in a moonlit forest, a place of enchantment. The title of the play suggests that it is all a dream—an illusion or fantasy that may disappear in the clear light of day. Meanwhile, the audience can sit back and enjoy mischievous and meddlesome spirits who interfere in the lives of mortals with some comic (and some temporarily tragic) results.

To be certain that you have sorted out all the problems presented in Act II, try answering the following questions.

1. What spoils the usually happy relationship between Oberon and Titania and causes them to quarrel?

   _____

2. Look again at Act II, Scene I, lines 90–114. What evils have happened to the world since Oberon and Titania have been quarreling? Name at least three.

   _____

3. According to Oberon, how did love-in-idleness gain its magic power (see lines 157–172)?

   _____

4. Out of anger, jealousy, or spite, Oberon sprinkles the flower juice on Titania's eyelids, hoping that she will awaken and fall in love with someone completely unsuitable. Why does he send Puck to sprinkle the potion on Demetrius's eyelids?

   _____

5. What error does Puck make? What are the consequences? _____

   _____

6. At the end of Act II, what is the state of mind of each of the four young lovers?

   Helena _____

   Lysander _____

   Demetrius _____

   Hermia _____

Reading Quiz: *A Midsummer Night's Dream,* **Act II**

A Midsummer Night's Dream contains some of Shakespeare's most beautiful writing. This quiz will test your understanding of his language and your diligence in reading the footnotes.

1. What actual person of Shakespeare's time does the fairy queen, Titania, represent? (*Hint:* This was a very important person, one Shakespeare would have wanted to please.)

    _____

2. The fairy, talking with Puck, says of Titania,

    > *The cowslips tall her pensioners be;*
    > *In their gold coats spots you see . . .*

    Cowslips are better known as dog-toothed violets in the United States. In these two lines, the cowslips are described as if they were human beings, "pensioners," in uniform (gold coats). How do you think the "pensioners" are connected to the person you named in question 1?

    _____

3. When Oberon meets Titania, he says, "Ill met by moonlight, proud Titania." Put the first four words of his speech into your own words. (*Hint:* Moonlight is often associated with lovers; is it used in that sense here?)

    _____

4. When Oberon tells Puck to hurry on his errand to get the magic flower, Puck replies, "I'll put a girdle round about the earth in forty minutes." In your own words, what is Puck boasting that he will do?

    _____

5. In describing the flowery bank where Titania lies sleeping, Oberon says,

    > *And there the snake throws his enamell'd skin,*
    > *Weed wide enough to wrap a fairy in.*

    You know that snakes shed their skins, and your footnote probably told you that in one sense, *weed* means *garment*. We refer to widow's *weeds* when a woman dresses all in black after her husband's death. In your own words, what is Oberon saying about a possible use of the snakeskin?

    _____

What Happens in Act III, *A Midsummer Night's Dream*

Act III, Scene I Titania is asleep on a flower-strewn bank when the artisans appear, discussing their play. Fearing that it may be too violent for the ladies, they decide to make certain changes in it, adding two characters, Moonshine and Wall.

Puck appears, unseen by the artisans, and plays a trick by putting an ass's head on Bottom the weaver. When the others see him, they flee, leaving poor Bottom alone and unaware of their reason for deserting him.

To keep his courage up, he sings, awakening Titania. The magic potion has done its work; she falls in love with Bottom immediately. He can't believe that she could love him and hopes only to find his way out of the forest. She says he must stay and promises that her fairies will take care of him. Four come to do her bidding, to feed Bottom and guard him while he sleeps. He is confused but is polite to his new servants.

Act III, Scene II Oberon is wondering if Titania has already awakened when Puck comes in to tell him about a trick he played on Bottom and the others. As a result, Titania has fallen in love with an ass! Oberon then wants to know if Puck was successful in putting the love potion on the young Athenian's eyelids. Puck says he was, and at that moment, Demetrius and Hermia appear. Oberon recognizes Demetrius as the man whose conversation with Helena he overheard. Puck, on the other hand, recognizes Hermia but not Demetrius and realizes that he has anointed the wrong man's eyelids.

The two young people argue. Demetrius is still trying to win Hermia. She accuses him of murdering Lysander, for she is certain that he would never willingly have left her while she slept. Demetrius denies having killed his rival, but she does not believe him and goes off in anger. Tired and discouraged, Demetrius lies down to sleep.

Oberon chastises Puck for his mistake in anointing Lysander instead of Demetrius. He then sends Puck to find Helena and bring her back. Meanwhile, Oberon will sprinkle the love juice on Demetrius' eyelids. When he awakens, he will see Helena and all will be well.

Puck returns with both Helena and Lysander. Lysander is still begging Helena to love him, and she still doubts him. Far from regretting his mistake, Puck says that he is going to enjoy the spectacle of two men trying to win one woman.

Demetrius wakes up, sees Helena, and immediately tells her how beautiful she is. She thinks that he, like Lysander, is simply mocking her, and she accuses both of being unmanly in their behavior.

Lysander, assuming that Demetrius still truly loves Hermia, asks to have Helena for himself. Demetrius, in turn, tells Lysander to take Hermia, for Helena is now his beloved.

Hermia, who has been searching for Lysander, hears his voice and comes toward the others, asking Lysander why he left her. Coldly, he says that it was because he does not love her; Helena has his love. Hermia doubts his words, and Helena, thinking that Hermia is part of the plot to mock her, reminds Hermia that they have always been like sisters. How then, she says, could Hermia have joined the men in humiliating her?

Hermia is confused by Helena's speech, and Helena, unhappy, tries to leave, but both men beg her to stay, each declaring his love. The men then threaten each other. Lysander tells Hermia that he hates her, and Hermia turns on Helena, thinking that she has stolen Lysander's love. Hermia wants to fight, but Helena is timid. The men vow to protect her from Hermia, but they leave together, and the two women are alone. Helena leaves hastily to avoid a fight.

(continued)

What Happens in Act III, *A Midsummer Night's Dream* (continued)

Puck and the fairies

Oberon accuses Puck of having deliberately anointed the wrong man, but Puck assures him that it was a mistake. Oberon tells him to follow the two Athenians. When Lysander tires and falls asleep, Puck is to drop a second herb on his eyelids, this one a cure for the first. When he awakens, he will love Hermia again, and all that has happened will seem like a dream. Oberon, meanwhile, will go to his Titania, beg her for the mortal boy, and apply the herb that will release her from her love for Bottom.

Puck, invisible, goes back to Lysander and Demetrius, speaking to each in the voice of the other and stirring up more anger while he leads them hither and yon. Finally, tired of the futile chase, Lysander lies down to rest, and a little later Demetrius does the same. Helena comes along, weary and unhappy. She lies down and goes to sleep. Puck now has three of the four lovers together, although they do not know it. Hermia arrives, weary and still concerned that any harm might have come to Lysander from Demetrius. Puck squeezes onto Lysander's eyes the herb that is the cure for the first potion. The act ends with Puck saying that all will now be well and that "Jack shall have Jill."

         The Complete Guide to Shakespeare's Best Plays

Lesson 33: A Closer Look at the Characters

So far in the play, you have been asked to concentrate on the twists and turns of the plot. In this lesson, you will take a closer look at the characters. It is part of Shakespeare's genius as a writer that he is able to make even the minor characters "come alive" so that they seem like real people.

Let's begin with a few of those minor characters, the artisans.

1. In Act I, Scene II, the artisans meet to assign parts for *Pyramus and Thisby*. Who seems to be in charge? _____

   What work did he do to prepare for the meeting? _____
   _____

   What task will he perform before the artisans meet again? _____
   _____

2. Which of the actors seems eager to play every part? _____
   (This same actor gives quite a bit of advice to the man discussed in the answer to question 1.)

3. Snug the joiner is assigned the part of the lion. What is his immediate concern? _____
   _____

   What does that show about his abilities? _____
   _____

4. You meet Bottom the weaver again in Act III, when Puck plays a trick on him and Queen Titania falls in love with him. Look again at Act III, Scene I, lines 146–150, in which Bottom makes a very shrewd observation, and Titania calls him wise. Does his speech here change your opinion of him in any way? Explain.
   _____
   _____

5. Bottom says he can "gleek" upon occasion. *Gleek* means jest or joke. Do you find any evidence to support his claim in this scene? If so, give an example.
   _____

6. In your opinion, what one adjective best describes each of the following spirits? (*Hint:* Think of their actions. For example, which one or ones show concern for others?)

   Titania _____

   Oberon _____

   Puck _____

7. Now for the lovers. Shakespeare allows us to see the women through others' eyes.

   Which one is the greater beauty? _____

   Which one is tall and stately? _____

   As for Lysander and Demetrius, do you agree with Helena that they are unmanly in their behavior toward women? Explain.
   _____
   _____
   _____

Reading Quiz: *A Midsummer Night's Dream,* **Act III**

1. At the opening of the play, Demetrius and Lysander both love Hermia, Hermia loves Lysander, and Helena loves Demetrius. Fill in the blanks below to show how the relationships have changed.

   Demetrius now loves _____

   Lysander now loves _____

   Helena now loves _____

   Hermia now loves _____

2. Who are Peaseblossom, Cobweb, Moth, and Mustardseed? _____

   _____

3. When Puck says that they must conclude their work quickly because it is almost dawn ("Yonder shines Aurora's harbinger"), and spirits disappear with the coming of the day, what is Oberon's reply?

   _____

4. Why isn't Helena delighted that Demetrius is now declaring his love for her? _____

   _____

5. What causes the falling out between Helena and Hermia? _____

   _____

What Happens in Act IV, *A Midsummer Night's Dream*

Act IV, Scene I While the four young lovers are still sleeping, Titania, her attendants, and Bottom appear. She speaks lovingly to Bottom. He asks Peaseblossom and Mustardseed to scratch his head for him, complaining that he is very hairy about the face and needs a barber. Obviously, he is still unaware that he is wearing an ass's head. Titania offers him music and food, but he wants oats and hay. Then he begins to feel sleepy, and both he and Titania fall asleep.

Puck joins Oberon, who has been hiding and watching. Oberon tells Puck that he has already had a meeting with Titania and that she has given him the child. Now feeling sorry for her, Oberon decides to awaken her from her spell. He instructs Puck to remove the ass's head from Bottom, who will then return to Athens believing that the night's events were only a dream.

When Oberon wakes Titania, she thinks that she dreamt of being in love with an ass. Oberon calls for music to soothe her, and he invites her to dance. He predicts that the two of them will dance at Theseus's wedding and that the other two pairs of lovers will be married during that celebration. He and Titania then depart.

Theseus comes in with his bride-to-be and Hermia's father, Egeus. The duke tells his forester to arrange a hunt for Hippolyta's entertainment. She mentions a hunt in Crete, where she was very impressed by the hounds of Sparta. Theseus boasts that no dogs can compete with his.

At that point, he notices the four young lovers still asleep. Egeus is quite surprised to find them together, but Theseus says that they have probably come to observe the rites of May. Then he recalls that this was the day when Hermia was to decide whether or not she would marry Demetrius.

The hunters' horns awaken the sleepers. Theseus asks why they are all together. Respectfully, Lysander explains that he and Hermia were running away from Athens and Athenian law.

Egeus immediately wants to bring the force of the law upon Lysander's head. Then Demetrius explains that he came to the forest after hearing of Lysander and Hermia's elopement. In anger, he has been following them, and Helena has been following *him*. Then, by some strange coincidence, he has become indifferent to Hermia and in love once more with Helena, to whom he was originally engaged.

Glad of a peaceful solution, Theseus tells Egeus that he is not going to punish the lovers. In fact, he wants the two couples to be married on his and Hippolyta's wedding day. He and his followers then leave.

Now alone, the four young people try to sort out what happened. Did they dream, and are they still dreaming? Was the duke really there? Still confused, they decide to return to Athens.

When Bottom wakes up, he thinks that he is still rehearsing the play. Then he remembers his "dream" and is so puzzled by it that he hesitates to describe his experience. Finally, he decides to have Peter Quince write a ballad about it, to be called "Bottom's Dream." Bottom plans to sing it for the duke.

Act IV, Scene II At Quince's house, he and the other artisans are concerned because Bottom is missing. Without him, they cannot perform the play. Snug comes in to say that the duke's wedding and that of "two or three lords and ladies more" have just taken place. Flute regrets that Bottom, by his absence, has probably lost a life's pension, for surely the duke would have rewarded him for his performance. At that point, Bottom arrives. He refuses to talk of his adventure and urges them to prepare for the play. He also gives them a few hints about acting.

Lesson 34: The Enchanted Wood

Although Oberon, Titania, and Puck have human characteristics—good and bad—they are, after all, spirits. In the city of Athens, in the cold light of day, they might seem quite out of place, but in the enchanted wood, lit only by moonbeams, they are more believable. Love potions and their cures; a beautiful fairy queen in love with the most ordinary of mortals, and one who wears an ass's head at that; young people who fall in and out of love at the blink of an eye; all these seem far removed from the real world, but in the half light of the forest, anything is possible.

It is part of Shakespeare's skill as a dramatist that he has created a setting so perfectly suited to the action of the play. It is important to remember, though, that in the theater of Shakespeare's day few props were used, and the stage itself was nearly bare. Thus the audience had to depend on imagination and Shakespeare's wonderful word pictures to help them imagine the setting. Let's examine a few of those word pictures now.

At various times in various parts of the wood, the following descriptions are given. In each case, through whose eyes are we viewing the setting? (Refer back to the text if you must, but first try to figure out the answers for yourself.)

1. **Act II, Scene I**

   I know a bank where the wild thyme blow
   Where oxslips, the nodding violet grow,
   Quite over-canopied with luscious woodbine,
   With sweet musk rose and with eglantine . . .

   Who is the speaker? _____

   Whose bed in the forest is he describing? _____

2. **Act III, Scene I**

   This green plot shall be our stage, this
   hawthorne brake our tiring house. *   *dressing room

   Who is the speaker? _____

   Of what group is he a member? _____

3. **Act III, Scene I**

   Be kind and courteous to this gentleman . . .
   Feed him with apricocks and dewberries,
   With purple grapes, green figs and mulberries;
   The honey bags steal from the humble bees . . .
   And pluck the wings from painted butterflies
   To fan the moonbeams from his sleeping eyes.

   Who is the speaker? _____

   Who is being instructed? _____

   Who is "this gentleman"? _____

4. *My fairy lord, this must be done with haste,*
   For night's swift dragons cut the clouds full fast,
   And yonder shines Aurora's harbinger.

   Who is the speaker? _____

   What time of night or day is it? _____

Name _____ Date _____

Reading Quiz: *A Midsummer Night's Dream,* **Act IV**

This play was one of Shakespeare's earliest. It was written primarily to entertain with music, plays on words, and humor provided by the artisans, who behave like clowns. Nevertheless, it has some memorable lines worthy of our close attention.

1. Probably the best known of those lines is:
The course of true love never did run smooth,
spoken by Lysander to Hermia early in the play. First restate Lysander's comment in your own words. Then briefly outline how events in the play illustrate the truth of his statement. Use the back of this paper to complete your answer.

_____

_____

2. In this quotation Bottom speaks to Titania, who has just told him she loves him:
Reason and love keep little company together now-a-days.
He might have said, "The heart often rules the head." Remember that Bottom is supposed to be a simple person. Do you think he shows wisdom in this speech? Explain.

_____

_____

Do you find Bottom pathetic here? If so, why? _____

_____

3. Finally, here is a quotation from Puck, one you may have heard before:
Lord, what fools these mortals be.
Keeping in mind that Oberon and Puck have caused the problems in the play, do you think his statement is fair? Explain.

_____

_____

4. If you were to choose a single adjective to describe Oberon, Puck, or Titania, which one would you choose? (*Hint:* In question 3, you have a good example of Puck's view of the world. Think of Oberon's overall behavior to Titania and his concern for those lovers at cross-purposes. Think of Titania's concern about the consequences of her quarrel with Oberon.)

Puck—*adj.* _____

Oberon—*adj.* _____

Titania—*adj.* _____

What Happens in Act V, *A Midsummer Night's Dream*

Act V, Scene I Hippolyta and Theseus discuss the strange story told by the four young lovers, Demetrius, Helena, Lysander, and Hermia, Theseus dismisses it as a figment of their imagination, but because everyone has told the same story, Hippolyta is inclined to believe it.

The lovers come in. After greeting them, Theseus calls for his master of revels (festivities), Philostrate, to ask him what entertainment is planned for the evening. From the list of proposed performances, Theseus chooses *Pyramus and Thisby* because its description as both merry and tragic amuses him. Philostrate is afraid that the actors, ordinary workmen with no previous acting experience, may not perform well, but Theseus is certain that since their intentions are the best, he will enjoy their play,

Hippolyta too is afraid the play will be a disappointment, but Theseus assures her that the effort the artisans will make is what counts. Their sincere attempt to please will make their performance enjoyable.

Quince offers a muddled prologue (introduction) to the play, introduces the players, and then goes on to tell the story before it is even performed. Wall, played by Snout, then makes his speech, amusing the spectators. Pyramus comes in and speaks to Wall, but when Duke Theseus makes an aside, Pyramus speaks directly to him. Next comes a meeting between Pyramus and Thisby, the lovers, who agree to meet at "Ninny's tomb." They leave, followed by Wall, who explains to the audience that he has done his part.

Hippolyta complains that the play is silly, but Theseus says that the best of actors are but shadows, and the worst, no less. Imagination is all that is needed to enjoy the play.

Lion and Moonshine come in, explaining their roles to the audience. Then Thisby returns but is frightened by Lion and runs off. Lion shakes Thisby's mantle (cloak) before running off, too. Pyramus returns, sees Thisby's bloody cloak, assumes she is dead, and stabs himself. Meanwhile, the members of the wedding party, finding the play amusing, comment among themselves. Thisby returns to the stage, sees Pyramus dead, delivers a speech that none of the watchers could possibly take seriously, and then stabs herself.

As Theseus and Demetrius talk, Bottom comes back to life to offer them a choice of an epilogue (ending speech) or a Bergomask (or rustic) dance. Theseus chooses the dance. As soon as the entertainment is over, all leave.

It is now late at night, when all sorts of strange things occur, and the fairies are about to begin their nightly revels. Puck appears, followed shortly by Oberon, Titania, and their followers. They sing, dance, and bless the place so that the three newlywed couples will have good luck.

Finally, all depart except Puck. He speaks to the members of the audience, telling them that if the play has offended, they are to think of it only as a dream, a midsummer night's dream. He asks them to applaud if they are his and the actors' friends.

© 1985, 2000 J. Weston Walch, Publisher 97 *The Complete Guide to Shakespeare's Best Plays*

Lesson 35:
Shakespeare's Message in *A Midsummer Night's Dream*

The play you have just read was written early in Shakespeare's career as a dramatist, probably about 1594 or 1595. It is truly a comedy, with all the lovers reunited in the end, presumably to live happily ever after. It has broad comedy as well in the clumsy but earnest performance of *Pyramus and Thisby* by the artisans. But Shakespeare also has some serious lines in the play, lines that show what he believed was the role of the poet or the dramatist. (Remember that much of the dialogue in his plays is in blank verse, and much of *A Midsummer Night's Dream* has rhyming verse.)

In this lesson, you are asked to look closely at 16 lines of poetry that appear in Act V, Scene I, lines 7–22, and paraphrase (put into your own words) the meaning of those lines. First:

The lunatic, the lover, and the poet
Are of imagination all compact.

For *lunatic* you might want to substitute *madman*. *Compact* in this sense means *composed* or *formed*. Move the prepositional phrase "of imagination" to the end of the line and you have "Are all compact (composed) of imagination." Now write the two lines as a sentence in the space below.

1. _____

Let's try the next few lines:

One sees more devils than vast hell can hold:
That is the madman. The lover, all as frantic,
Sees Helen's beauty in a brow of Egypt,
The poet's eye, in a fine frenzy rolling,
Doth glance from heaven to earth, from earth to heaven . . .

2. In the first line, substitute *The madman* for *One* and paraphrase.

_____

_____

3. In the description of the lover, find your own phrase to replace "all as frantic." *Helen* refers to Helen of Troy, a very beautiful woman, and *Egypt* refers to a gypsy. Here, *brow* is a kind of shorthand for her whole face. Now put into your own words what Shakespeare says about the lover.

_____

_____

4. Finally we come to the description of the poet. Remember that Shakespeare was a poet. Thus, he is describing himself. Try compressing his eighteen words into about eight, keeping the meaning.

_____

_____

The rest of the quotation is a description of what imagination can do. Read it first, remembering to read by punctuation, not line endings. The passage will then become clearer to you.

And as imagination bodies forth
The forms of things unknown, the poet's pen
Turns them to shapes, and gives to airy nothing
A local habitation and a name.
Such tricks hath strong imagination,
That, if it would but apprehend some joy,
It comprehends some bringer of that joy;
Or in the night, imagining some fear,
How easy is a bush suppos'd a bear!

(continued)

Lesson 35:
Shakespeare's Message in *A Midsummer Night's Dream* (continued)

5. In the first four lines, what is Shakespeare saying the imagination is capable of doing? _____

_____

_____

What does it have to do with making things seem real? _____

_____

_____

In the last five lines, imagination seems to have both a positive and a negative side, bringing both joy and fear. Before you paraphrase below, check the meanings of *apprehend* and *comprehend* to be certain you know the difference.

6. Paraphrase the last five lines: _____

_____

_____

_____

7. Finally, do you agree with Shakespeare about the power of imagination? Explain.

_____

_____

_____

_____

_____

Name _____ Date _____

Reading Quiz: *A Midsummer Night's Dream,* **Act V**

1. Of the members of the audience, who is most sympathetic to the artisans as they present their play?

   _____

2. Who is the least sympathetic, calling the play silly?

   _____

3. What is a Bergomask? _____

4. Who is the speaker of these lines? _____

   Now the wasted brands do glow
   Whilst the screech owl, screeching loud,
   Puts the wretch that lies in woe
   In remembrance of a shroud.

   What time of day or night is it? _____

5. In the play within a play, why does Pyramus kill himself? _____

   _____

Final Test: *A Midsummer Night's Dream*

After the name of each character below, write the letter of the adjective that best describes her or him. You may write more than one letter after a character's name.

Characters	Adjectives

Characters

1. Theseus _____
2. Hippolyta _____
3. Lysander _____
4. Hermia _____
5. Demetrius _____
6. Helena _____
7. Egeus _____
8. Bottom _____
9. Quince _____
10. Oberon _____
11. Titania _____
12. Puck _____

Adjectives

A. basically kind but jealous
B. naturally loving and concerned for others' welfare
C. vengeful
D. calm and just
E. resourceful, but not hesitant to tell tales
F. somewhat inconstant in love
G. an organizer, in charge of the play within a play
H. short in stature but very beautiful
I. tall and timid
J. overly sure of his own abilities, but capable of flashes of wisdom
K. mischievous
L. firmly ground in reality
M. lacking in patience with others' lack of skill and polish
N. scornful of mortals

13. Which character said, "The course of true love never did run smooth?"

_____

14. Which character said, "Lord, what fools these mortals be!"? _____

15. What famous person of Shakespeare's day is Titania said to represent?

_____

16. Why have Oberon and Titania quarreled? _____

17. In Shakespeare's time, if a young woman refused the man her father chose for her, how was

she punished? _____

18. What does Bottom warn the other actors not to eat before they present the play? Why does he

give that warning? _____

19. Which character in the play interested you the most? Why? _____

_____

20. **Bonus Item**

What quality do the lunatic, the lover, and the poet have in common?
Why do you think Shakespeare would have seen that quality as very important?

To the Teacher:

Suggestions for Presenting *The Tempest*

Sources

Although high school students might not be particularly interested in the variety of sources Shakespeare used for his plays, it is worthwhile to point out that his plots generally were not original but were based on earlier stories. Thus the audience of his day knew how the play would end, but they were still very interested in his way of telling the story.

Among the sources for *The Tempest* were two accounts published in 1610 of an actual shipwreck the previous year. The *Sea Venture* had left England, bound for the colonies in Virginia, with several dignitaries and some settlers aboard. A storm drove the ship from its course, and it was wrecked off Bermuda. Everyone survived. They spent several months on the island, building two smaller vessels from the wreckage of the original. These eventually carried them to Virginia.

Introducing the Play

Before reading this or any other play by Shakespeare, students should review Lessons 1 and 2, "Getting Acquainted with Shakespeare" and "Shakespeare's London." For further reading, Marchette Chute's *Shakespeare of London* is a good source. Also, as an introduction to the plays, the video *Looking for Richard* with Al Pacino is worth viewing.

Encourage students to get into the habit of reading any footnotes. This will help them understand the action and will increase their vocabularies as well, for many unfamiliar words may be footnoted.

It is worthwhile to review vocabulary after reading each act. Such a review could be based on word lists the students have made in their notebooks. Also, discuss key words such as *usurp*, which appears first in the *Dramatis Personae*.

Reading the Play

Ask the students to take parts and read some of the play aloud in class, paying close attention to punctuation rather than line endings. Listening to recordings of the play will help the students understand the language. Screening a film version of the play as a culminating activity allows students to compare an actual performance with their imagined staging of the play.

Special Exercises

Allow students to choose from among the following exercises.

A. Write an essay describing your reaction to a custom revealed in the play, such as Prospero's setting up the meeting between Miranda and Ferdinand so that they will fall in love. He is actually arranging their marriage.

B. Work with a small group to present to the class a brief scene from the play.

C. Work with a group to construct a model of the Globe Theater (pictured in many texts).

D. Work with a small group to create a poster advertising a performance of *The Tempest*.

What Happens in Act I, *The Tempest*

Act I, Scene I The play begins aboard ship during a violent storm. The ship's master tells the boatswain (a ship's officer) to summon the crew quickly to tend the sails, or the ship will surely go aground.

Several passengers (King Alonso and some of his noblemen) come on deck and get in the way of the crew. The boatswain tries to send them below. Gonzalo, the king's counselor, reminds the boatswain of the passengers' importance, but he is unimpressed. To make matters worse, Sebastian (the king's brother) and Antonio (who has stolen the title of duke of Milan) try to heckle the boatswain. He ignores them and continues to direct the crew. Only when several sailors rush in to say that the ship is sinking do Gonzalo, Sebastian, and Antonio go below to join the king and prince at their prayers.

Act I, Scene II On an island, Prospero, the rightful duke of Milan, talks with his daughter, Miranda. She urges him to calm the sea, saying that she has just seen a ship dashed to pieces. She assumes that everyone aboard is lost. Prospero, who has supernatural powers, assures her that no one aboard the ship is injured. He directs her to remove his magical cloak, for he has something to tell her.

Prospero reminds Miranda that the island has been their home for twelve years and that they arrived on it when she was only three. Before they came to the island, however, he was the powerful duke of Milan, but because he was interested in certain "secret studies," he left the task of governing to his trusted brother, Antonio.

Given such an opportunity, Antonio took the revenues (money) that should have gone to Prospero, and by various means won the support of those who should have been loyal to Prospero.

Antonio then joined with Prospero's enemy, the king of Naples, promising him "tribute" (money) and "homage" (faithful service). In return, he asked the king to arrange to get rid of Prospero and Miranda. This the king did.

They were kidnapped and put aboard a leaky boat with little hope of survival, but Gonzalo, who had been ordered to carry out the actual kidnapping, took pity on them and provided them with food, water, clothing, and books from Prospero's own library. Thus, Prospero explains to Miranda, he was able to educate her even though Providence had brought them to this remote island.

Having heard his story, Miranda is still curious as to why her father "raised" (brought about) the storm. He says only that by good fortune, his enemies are now on the island. He claims that his success will depend on whether or not he makes the right moves. He will explain no further and tells her to go to sleep. She does.

Ariel, a spirit who does Prospero's bidding, enters and explains that, carrying out Prospero's orders, he has caused fires to break out all over the ship, so frightening the passengers that they all jumped into the ocean. Ariel has "dispersed" (scattered) them to various points on the island, leaving Prince Ferdinand by himself. As for the crew and the ship, both are safely hidden in a cove. The sailors are asleep; the other ships that were part of the convoy are returning to Naples, assuming the king's ship is lost.

Prospero has more work for Ariel, who complains that he wants his promised freedom. Angry, Prospero reminds him that he was once in the service of a wicked witch, Sycorax. She confined him in a cloven pine, where he was forced to remain a dozen years until Prospero freed him. (The witch is now dead, but her offspring, Caliban, lives on the island and serves Prospero.) Prospero is capable of confining Ariel just as Sycorax did unless he carries out Prospero's orders.

Ariel agrees to do whatever Prospero asks. In exchange, Prospero promises him that he will have his freedom in two days. Meanwhile, he is to take the form of a water nymph but remain invisible to everyone except his master. Ariel leaves just as Miranda awakens.

(continued)

What Happens in Act I, *The Tempest* (continued)

Prospero tells Miranda they will meet Caliban. She is reluctant, but Prospero points out that Caliban does perform all their menial tasks. He calls the slave, using harsh words. Caliban comes forward, cursing them. For his rudeness, Prospero says he will be punished.

Caliban complains that the island was his before Prospero and Miranda arrived. He showed Prospero where to find freshwater springs and fertile soil. In return, he is treated as a servant and confined to a rocky corner of the island. Angry, Prospero reminds the evil creature that he was treated kindly, taught to speak, and allowed to live with them until he tried to rape Miranda. It is clear that Caliban is no match for Prospero and his spells. Grumbling, he goes off to gather wood.

Ariel, invisible, enters, followed by Prince Ferdinand. Ariel sings, and Ferdinand recognizes the strange music that he has heard earlier and has followed to this place. Meanwhile, Prospero asks Miranda to look at Ferdinand. She is pleased and thinks at first that he is a spirit, but her father assures her that he is human.

Ferdinand, in turn, looks at Miranda. He thinks that she is a goddess and asks her if she is mortal or immortal. She assures him that she is human. He is astonished that she speaks his language, the language of Naples. He says that he is now king of Naples because his father and all his followers were lost in the shipwreck.

Prospero, noting that the young people are charmed with each other, decides not to make things too easy for them. He fears that if he does, they will not truly appreciate their good fortune. He accuses Ferdinand of being a spy and of trying to steal his island from him. He then causes a quarrel with the prince, who tries to draw his sword. Prospero, however, has cast a spell on the prince, and he cannot move. Miranda tries to take Ferdinand's part, but her father brushes her aside. Ferdinand, although exhausted by all of the

strange things that have happened to him, and realizing that he is powerless against Prospero, still vows that even in prison he could survive if once a day he could "behold" Miranda.

Name _____ Date _____

Lesson 36: Parallels and Personalities

The Tempest, the last of Shakespeare's plays, is among his greatest. Certainly, in the first act enough tension is created to keep the audience (or a reader) interested in seeing how it is all going to "come out." First there is the apparent shipwreck. Then two principal characters are introduced: Prospero, a mortal with supernatural powers, and Miranda, his beautiful daughter. She has been isolated from all human beings except her remarkable father and the brutish Caliban. Next comes Ariel, a supernatural creature who does the bidding of a mortal, Prospero. Then there is Prospero's story of how his brother betrayed him. Finally, an apparent coincidence brings Ferdinand, the son of Prospero's enemy, the king of Naples, into Miranda's presence. The result is a case of "love at first sight" for the two young people.

1. You may recognize in the plot of *The Tempest* parallels or similarities to earlier plays.

   A. In what other play does a brother seize the power of the rightful ruler? (*Hint:* In the other play, brother murders brother. In *The Tempest*, Antonio simply sets up a situation that will probably result in Prospero's and Miranda's death by drowning.)

   _____

   B. In what other play do two young people fall in love at first sight, even though their fathers are

   enemies? _____

   C. In what other play do spirits interfere with mortals? (In that play, the spirits interfere on their own. In *The Tempest*, Ariel interferes while carrying out Prospero's orders.)

   _____

2. Shakespeare, a firm believer in the right of kings and queens to rule, shows in several of his plays that if the rightful ruler is deposed, chaos results. Prospero's dukedom has been taken over by Antonio, who puts Milan under the rule of the king of Naples. Is Prospero entirely blameless for what has happened to Milan? (*Hint:* Think of why Antonio took over the government.)

   _____

3. In the first act, you meet Caliban, a brutish lout, a slave to Prospero, resentful of the man whose orders he must obey. Does Caliban have any good features? (*Hint:* Remember what he did for Prospero when he and Miranda first arrived on the island.)

   _____

4. How would you describe Prospero's character?

   _____

   _____

5. What kind of person does Caliban represent?

   _____

6. From what little you have seen of Ferdinand, what adjectives would you use to describe him?

   _____

   _____

7. What adjectives would you use to describe Miranda? _____

   _____

Reading Quiz: *The Tempest,* **Act I**

1. When the play opens, what dramatic event is taking place?

   _____

   _____

2. What is the attitude of some of the ship's passengers toward the boatswain?

   _____

   _____

3. Despite their being marooned on an island, how has Prospero been able to educate his daughter?

   _____

   _____

4. When Ferdinand meets Prospero and Miranda, he tells them he is the king of Naples. Is that true? Explain.

   _____

   _____

5. Who on the island seems to represent evil?

   _____

   _____

What Happens in Act II, *The Tempest*

Act II, Scene I The other victims of the shipwreck, including Prospero's brother, Antonio, and Ferdinand's father, Alonso, king of Naples, are talking about their difficult situation. Gonzalo is thankful that they have escaped with their lives. He thinks that the island is fertile enough to survive there. One lord, Adrian, agrees, but Sebastian and Antonio refuse to take Gonzalo's comment seriously.

The king is very unhappy. He laments that his daughter, having married the king of Tunis, is gone from Naples, and he fears that his son has been lost in the shipwreck. Sebastian, his brother, doesn't help, saying that Alonso arranged his daughter's marriage; it is his own fault that she is in Tunis. Francisco gives the king some hope that Prince Ferdinand is still alive, for he has seen him swimming strongly toward shore.

Gonzalo tries to distract the king from his gloomy thoughts by suggesting that the island could become an ideal kingdom. The people would be innocent and pure, free from all the problems of the civilized world. Nature would provide. No one would need to work. No one would be in want. Antonio and Sebastian, always pessimistic, make fun of Gonzalo's idea, and the king tells him to speak no more about it.

Ariel comes in unseen and plays music that puts most of the people to sleep. Only the king, his brother Sebastian, and Antonio remain wakeful. Soon Alonso too is asleep.

The other two talk seriously. Antonio suggests to Sebastian that he could be king. Sebastian protests that Antonio must be talking in his sleep; still he wants to hear more. Antonio believes that Ferdinand has drowned, and Sebastian also has no hope for the prince. Antonio then talks about the succession to the throne. Claribel, the king's daughter, now lives in Tunis, too far from Naples to be the ruler. Sebastian could become king in his brother's place, just as Antonio himself became duke in Prospero's place. Only Alonso stands between Sebastian and the throne. Antonio is willing to kill Alonso as he sleeps, and Sebastian agrees to kill Gonzalo. They are about to do the wicked deeds when Ariel returns and sings in Gonzalo's ear, awakening him to danger. Alonso wakes also and sees the two conspirators with swords drawn. They explain that they have heard "a hollow burst of bellowing" and have drawn their swords to protect Alonso. Gonzalo admits that he too heard something, "a humming," which awakened him. Alonso then suggests that they move on and continue to search for Ferdinand. Ariel, still invisible, goes off to tell Prospero what has happened.

Act II, Scene II Meanwhile, in another part of the island, Caliban is gathering wood and cursing his master, Prospero, who, Caliban says, sends spirits to torture him. Trinculo, the jester, appears. Caliban, thinking that he is another of his master's spirits sent to tease him, falls down on the ground, hoping not to be noticed. Trinculo sees Caliban and doesn't at first know what to make of this strange-looking being, but since a thunderstorm is brewing and he has no other shelter, he crawls under Caliban's cloak.

Stephano, a drunken butler who was also a victim of the supposed shipwreck, comes upon what appears to be a four-legged man (Caliban and Trinculo both under the cloak). He decides that a four-legged man would be a fine and curious gift to take back to the ruler of Naples. He is surprised that the creature speaks his language and decides to give it some of his wine to steady its nerves and stop its shaking. (Caliban has been begging not to be tormented, thinking that a Spirit has found him.)

Trinculo, recognizing Stephano's voice but believing that he has drowned, thinks spirits have possessed him and speaks aloud.

Stephano observes that the creature has not only four legs but also two heads that speak in different voices, and he decides to give wine to the second head as well.

(continued)

What Happens in Act II, *The Tempest* (continued)

After the storm

Trinculo recognizes Stephano. At first, each thinks the other is a spirit, but finally they convince themselves that they have survived the shipwreck. Caliban, meanwhile, thinks that Stephano is a god who has given him "celestial liquor," and he vows to serve him. The others, meanwhile, are explaining how they have escaped—Trinculo, a strong swimmer, was able to get to shore. Stephano rode on a barrel of wine that the sailors had thrown overboard. He has his precious barrel hidden in a cave. They are amused by drunken Caliban's promises to show them all the riches the island has to offer—bird's eggs, a variety of nuts, crabs, and other delicacies. They go with him, believing that they alone have survived the shipwreck.

Lesson 37: A Closer Look at the Minor Characters

It has been said that Shakespeare was a fine psychologist centuries before that branch of science began to be explored. He had a remarkable understanding of how the human mind works. Thus, even minor characters are carefully drawn so that the audience can see their capabilities and their motivations. In the first act, we are aware that Prospero has "engineered" the storm for his own purposes, but those purposes are not yet clear.

In Act II, Antonio and Sebastian, who earlier have seemed merely cynical or distrusting, turn out to be sinister. In this act, as well, we meet two minor characters, Trinculo and Stephano, who both are quick to make the most of an opportunity.

As for Caliban, Shakespeare gives us a better look at his character and succeeds in making us feel a little sorry for this strange, misshapen creature.

Also in Act II, Shakespeare gives the audience a little comic relief after the intensity of the first act. The spectacle of drunken Stephano gazing upon a strange creature that appears to have four legs would have amused Shakespeare's audience. The dialogue in this scene serves two purposes: it is entertaining, and it explains how Trinculo and Stephano escaped the shipwreck. (In other words, Shakespeare is filling in necessary details.)

Let's take a second look at the minor characters in Act II to explore their motivations.

Below is a list of adjectives. Choose the adjective or adjectives that best describes Caliban, Trinculo, and Stephano. Before you begin, you may want to check the dictionary for the exact meaning of each adjective.

servile   starved for kindness
generous   ingenious
practical   opportunistic
humble

1. **Characters**   **Adjectives**

   Trinculo _____

   Caliban _____

   Stephano _____

2. Caliban thinks that Stephano has "dropped from heaven." What does Stephano do that makes Caliban so eager to serve him?

   _____

3. When Stephano first comes upon the "four-legged" creature, why does he decide to take it back to Naples?

   _____

4. In talking to Trinculo about the "fact" that the king and all his followers have drowned, does Stephano show any regrets? Explain.

   _____

5. Trinculo's speech in Act II, Scene II, lines 169–170, "A most ridiculous monster, to make a wonder of a poor drunkard!" shows that he has a clear understanding of the situation. Who is the "poor drunkard"?

   _____

6. Elsewhere Trinculo says, "A most perfidious and drunken monster! when's [when his] God's [God is] asleep, he'll rob his bottle." Who is the monster, and what does Trinculo predict that he will do?

   _____

Name _____ Date _____

Reading Quiz: *The Tempest,* Act II

1. Does Antonio's conscience bother him because he has stolen his brother's dukedom?

   _____

2. Does Sebastian seem to have any serious misgivings about stealing Alonso's throne?

   _____

3. Why is Antonio willing to murder Alonso? In other words, what's in it for him?

   _____

   _____

4. Who prevents the double murder of Alonso and Gonzalo?

   _____

5. When Alonso wakes up, what excuse do Antonio and Sebastian give for having their swords drawn?

   _____

   _____

6. How does Gonzalo innocently support their lie?

   _____

   _____

(continued)

What Happens in Act III: *The Tempest*

Act III, Scene I On Prospero's orders, Prince Ferdinand is piling logs. He complains to himself of Prospero's harshness, but his task is made easier at the thought of Miranda, who would weep to see him at such hard labor.

Miranda then joins him, and Prospero stops nearby, out of sight of the two lovers. Miranda begs Ferdinand to rest, for her father is at his studies (or so she thinks) and will not bother them. She even offers to stack the logs for Ferdinand, but he will not permit it.

He asks Miranda what her name is, and she tells him. He tells her that he has always found some flaw in other women. She, however, is perfection.

In turn, Miranda explains that she doesn't know any other women. As for men, besides Ferdinand she knows only her father, but she is certain that Ferdinand is the man for her.

He says he is a prince and probably a king, but he hopes not. (If he is king, then his father is dead.) He would not do such menial work as Prospero has assigned, except for her sake.

Miranda asks him if he loves her. He assures her of his devotion. She, in turn, says she loves him and wants to be his wife. If he will not have her, then she will follow him and be his servant.

They seal their vows by shaking hands. They then say good-bye and leave separately. Prospero, who has heard the entire conversation, is pleased. He goes off to his studies.

Act III, Scene II Caliban, Trinculo, and Stephano are still together, drinking. Trinculo comments that there are only five people on the island. (He must have heard of Prospero and Miranda from Caliban.) He says that if the other two have no more brains than his drinking companions, then "the state totters" (things will not go well).

Caliban says that he will not serve Trinculo because he is not brave. Trinculo then belittles Caliban, who protests to Stephano. Stephano tells Trinculo to treat Caliban better.

Ariel arrives, invisible. Caliban talks of Prospero, who, he says, is a tyrant and a sorcerer (magician). Ariel says that he lies. Caliban protests, thinking that Trinculo has spoken. Stephano threatens Trinculo, who claims he did not speak.

Caliban claims that Prospero tricked him and stole the island from him. He ask Stephano to take revenge for him. Caliban offers to deliver Prospero to him, asleep, so that Stephano can drive a nail into his head. Ariel, still invisible, says that Caliban cannot do what he promises. Again, Caliban accuses Trinculo of interfering. Stephano threatens Trinculo, and Trinculo protests that he has done nothing. Again, Ariel answers, and Stephano, thinking that the voice is Trinculo's, begins to beat him. Trinculo assumes that drinking has caused Stephano's confusion.

Caliban explains that Prospero sleeps in the afternoon. Stephano can kill him then and seize the books, which are the source of Prospero's power. Caliban also says that Prospero has a beautiful daughter, who could become Stephano's wife.

Stephano sees himself as king of the island and Miranda as its queen. Caliban and Trinculo will be his viceroys. With such a happy future outlined, Stephano and Trinculo make peace with each other.

Stephano promises Caliban to murder Prospero in his sleep. Ariel, who has heard everything, is about to go off to tell Prospero. Caliban asks Stephano to sing the song he sang earlier. Stephano begins, but Caliban says the tune is not the same. Then they all hear music. (Ariel is the musician.) Stephano and Trinculo are frightened, but Caliban reassures them, saying the island is full of "sounds and sweet airs" but that no evil spirit will harm them. Stephano thinks that his new "kingdom" will be a fine place with free music. They all go off, following the sweet sounds.

(continued)

What Happens in Act III: *The Tempest* *(continued)*

Act III, Scene III Meanwhile, on another part of the island, Alonso and his courtiers are continuing their search for Ferdinand. Gonzalo finally protests that he is too weary to go on. Alonso says that he too is weary and despairing.

The two conspirators, Antonio and Sebastian, stand a bit away from the others. They decide that the murders must take place that night while Alonso and Gonzalo are too weary to be alert.

Suddenly everyone hears strange, sweet music. Prospero enters, invisible to the others, followed by several strangely shaped creatures carrying food. They dance about the food, gesturing to the king and his followers to eat. Then they disappear. The onlookers are confused. Alonso is reluctant to eat the food. Gonzalo tries to reassure him. Alonso decides to eat, for it doesn't matter to him now whether he lives or dies.

Ariel appears as a harpy (a monster with a woman's face and a vulture's body), claps his

wings, and the banquet vanishes. He then tells Alonso, Antonio, and Sebastian that the spirits will punish them. When those accused draw their swords, Ariel tells them that they are powerless against him and his fellow spirits. He vanishes, and Prospero, still invisible, comments that Ariel has done his bidding.

Now Prospero's enemies are distracted and in his power. Leaving them confused and worried, he returns to Miranda and Ferdinand.

Alonso thinks that he has heard the wind, the waves, and the thunder say Prospero's name. Certain that Ferdinand is drowned, he says that he will seek his son beneath the sea (will drown himself).

Antonio and Sebastian, still overconfident, think that they can fight the spirits. Gonzalo realizes that all three are desperate. He asks the younger courtiers to follow them to see that they don't get into any more trouble.

Lesson 38: "Power Tends to Corrupt"

The above quotation is from a nineteenth-century writer, Lord Acton. *The Tempest* seems to prove the truth of his statement. To begin with, Prospero turned over his power as duke of Milan to his brother, Antonio, who quickly allied himself with Alonso, king of Naples, and arranged for Prospero to be banished and probably sent to his death.

Prospero has great powers on the island where he and Miranda have lived for the past twelve years. Ariel and other spirits do his bidding. Caliban also is his slave and does what he is told.

Antonio and Sebastian plot to assassinate Alonso, king of Naples, who is Sebastian's brother. Thus Sebastian will gain power, for he will become king, or so he thinks, for he believes that Prince Ferdinand has drowned.

The urge to have power even affects the comic figures in the play, Stephano and Trinculo. Stephano has decided that he will become ruler of the island, with Trinculo and Caliban as his deputies. Trinculo evidently accepts that to be second in command is preferable to his present state.

Now let us examine the motivation of all these rulers and would-be rulers.

1. Prospero, as duke, had an obligation to his subjects to rule wisely and uphold Milan's position as an independent city-state. Did he fulfill his obligation? If not, why not?

   _____

2. Antonio, entrusted with the power that really belonged to Prospero, allied himself with Alonso, the king of Naples. What did Antonio hope to accomplish by that alliance?

   _____

3. Prospero masterminds everything that happens on or near his island, including the "shipwreck." Who actually carries out his plans?

   _____

   Caliban is Prospero's servant. How does Prospero treat Caliban? _____

   Contrast Prospero's treatment of Caliban with his treatment of Ariel. _____

   _____

   Caliban and Ariel have one thing in common—they both want their freedom from servitude. What might that desire show about their master's treatment of them?

   _____

   _____

4. Just as Antonio took his brother's place as duke of Milan, Sebastian intends to take Alonso's place as king of Naples. How exactly does Sebastian hope to gain the throne of Naples?

   _____

   Why does Antonio suggest that Sebastian take his brother's place? What does Antonio hope to gain?

   _____

5. Caliban likes Stephano and wants to serve him. Why is he so willing to desert his master, Prospero?

   _____

   Since he already has one loyal subject, Caliban, Stephano decides that he will rule the island and that Trinculo and Caliban will be his deputies. Why doesn't Trinculo challenge him for the higher post?

   _____

6. Who is the only underling in the play so far who remains loyal to his ruler and tries to take a positive view of the "shipwrecked" group's situation on the island?

   _____

Reading Quiz: *The Tempest,* **Act III**

1. In telling Stephano how and when to murder Prospero, Caliban also mentions the source of Prospero's remarkable powers. What is the source? (*Hint:* Remember what Caliban says Stephano must do before he attempts the murder.)

   _____

   _____

2. Ariel, the spirit who does Prospero's bidding, addresses certain members of the "shipwreck" party, calling them "three men of sin." Who are those three?

   _____

   _____

3. Gonzalo is a member of the "shipwreck" party, but he is very different from the other members of the party. What quality sets him apart?

   _____

   _____

4. At this point, does Alonso believe that Ferdinand is somewhere on the island? Explain.

   _____

   _____

5. Why do both Stephano and Trinculo refer to Caliban as a "monster"?

   _____

   _____

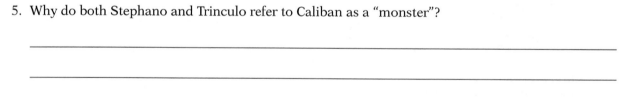

What Happens in Act IV, *The Tempest*

Act IV, Scene I Prospero explains to Ferdinand that the tasks he has had to perform were tests to see if he truly loved Miranda. Now Ferdinand has passed the tests and won Prospero's beloved daughter. He warns the prince that he must not make love to Miranda until they are married. Ferdinand assures Prospero that he has no cause to worry.

Ariel appears. Prospero praises him and his fellow spirits for carrying out the orders he gave them. He assigns a new task: Ariel is to bring Stephano, Trinculo, and Caliban to him.

When Ariel leaves, another spirit, Iris, comes forward and prays to Ceres, goddess of grain. Ceres is to come and join Juno, queen of the heavens and goddess of marriage. Ceres appears and asks Iris why Juno wants to see her. Iris asks her to bless the marriage of Miranda and Ferdinand and to give a gift to the lovers.

Ceres wants to know if Venus and Cupid will attend the festivities. She has a grudge against them for their plot to have Pluto capture Ceres' daughter and take her to the underworld. Iris assures Ceres that they will not attend.

Juno arrives. She and Ceres sing a song in which they bless Miranda and Ferdinand. Ferdinand asks Prospero if they are watching spirits. Prospero says that they are, summoned by his power to carry out his "present fancies." Ferdinand is very impressed.

Ceres and Juno give Iris another task, to summon the river nymphs and reapers. All appear and join in a dance until Prospero, remembering that Caliban, Trinculo, and Stephano are planning to kill him, dismisses the dancers.

Ferdinand and Miranda notice that Prospero is acting strangely, but he reassures them, saying the he has something to consider and needs to be alone. He sends the lovers away.

Ariel reappears and tells Prospero that the three would-be murderers are now in a slimy pool near Prospero's dwelling. Ariel has lured them there with music that they couldn't resist.

Prospero sends Ariel to bring back fancy clothing from the dwelling. Alone on the stage, Prospero speaks aloud. He thinks that Caliban is a devil on whom kindness is wasted. What's more, as Caliban grows older, he becomes uglier and more bitter.

Ariel returns with the fine garments and hangs them on a line. He and Prospero remain invisible as Caliban, Stephano, and Trinculo appear. The last two scold Caliban, annoyed after their dip in the pool. Caliban tries to soothe Stephano, his "master," and warns them to be quiet so that they can take Prospero by surprise. Trinculo notices the fancy clothing on the line, and he and Stephano begin putting on the garments. Caliban scolds them for wasting time and forgetting the deed they came to do.

More spirits appear, disguised as noisy hunting dogs and urged on by Prospero and Ariel. They succeed in driving the three would-be killers away. Prospero tells Ariel that now all his enemies are at his mercy, with Ariel's help. Only a little more work must be done, and Ariel will be free.

Lesson 39: Shakespeare's Message

You may be puzzled by the interludes in Act IV, when the spirits seem to take over end perform a little play (more properly called a *masque*) of their own. The interlude serves several purposes. First of all, the audience would have found it entertaining, just as we would enjoy a dance scene in a modern play. Also, the spirits' blessing of the marriage would have been a good omen to the people of Shakespeare's day. Further, the spirits are completely under Prospero's control. Shakespeare's contemporary audience would have accepted the idea of such power, and the use and abuse of power is an important theme of the play.

Act IV also contains a speech that scholars have read and reread, giving it various interpretations. It begins with Scene I, line 146:

You do look, my son, in a moved sort,
As if you were dismayed. Be cheerful, sir.

1. Prospero is commenting on Ferdinand's reaction to the spirits and telling him how he should be reacting. Now put those first two lines into your own words.

_____

_____

2. The next line is often analyzed and quoted. When Shakespeare says, "Our revels now are ended," does he mean simply that the spirits' country dance is all over and that Prospero must get on to more serious things, or does he mean that his days as a playwright and actor are over? (This was his last play.) Is he saying good-bye to the audience and the world of the theater? What do you think, and why?

_____

_____

_____

3. Prospero goes on, "These our actors . . . were all spirits and are melted into air, into thin air." Is he simply reassuring Ferdinand that what he has seen is a kind of dream? Or is he saying, as he does elsewhere in the plays, that we ourselves are like actors on the stage of life and then disappear (die)? What do you think, and why?

_____

_____

_____

4. In the next few lines, Shakespeare refers to artificial structures, such as towers, palaces, and temples, and then, "the great globe itself." What do you think he means by the "great globe"?

_____

What does he say will happen to it and all the buildings people have created?

_____

Does this view seem pessimistic to you? Explain. _____

_____

5. Finally, let's look at one more often-quoted sentence.

We are such stuff as dreams are made on,
And our little life is rounded with a sleep.

Put the sentence into your own words. Then try to describe your reaction to Shakespeare's version or your own. For example, does it make you sad?

_____

_____

_____

Reading Quiz: *The Tempest,* **Act IV**

1. After Caliban, Stephano, and Trinculo have been in the slimy pool, what do the last two complain that they have lost there?

   _____

   _____

2. In the conversation near Prospero's dwelling, when Stephano and Trinculo become interested in the fine clothes, what is Caliban's attitude? What does this reveal about his character?

   _____

   _____

3. Contrast briefly Prospero's attitude toward Ariel in this act with his overall attitude toward Caliban.

   _____

   _____

4. Aside from being a sorcerer, Prospero is a loving father. What warning does he give Ferdinand about his relationship with Miranda before their marriage?

   _____

   _____

5. **Bonus Item**

   In *A Midsummer Night's Dream,* Oberon and Titania, with their followers, go to Theseus's palace on the night of his wedding to Hippolyta. The fairies dance and sing and bless the house. What comparable activity takes place in Act IV of *The Tempest*?

   _____

   _____

What Happens in Act V, *The Tempest*

Act V, Scene I Outside his dwelling, Prospero asks Ariel what time it is. Ariel tells him that it is six o'clock, the time when their work was to have been finished. Prospero asks Ariel where the king of Naples and his followers are. Ariel says that they are not far from Prospero's house, confined by his magic. The king, his brother, Sebastian, and Prospero's brother, Antonio, are confused. Their followers, especially Gonzalo, are sorry to see them so distracted.

Prospero remembers the wrongs these three have committed, but since they are now regretful and confused, his reasonable nature overrides his anger. He instructs Ariel to release them. Prospero himself will remove the charms that have kept them captive.

Alone, Prospero addresses the spirits who have done his bidding, dimming the sun, raising strong winds, bringing the thunder, and performing other acts of magic. He tells them he will now break and bury his staff and throw his book into the ocean. (The staff and book are the symbols of his great powers.) In other words, he will no longer perform feats of magic.

Ariel returns with King Alonso and his counselor, Gonzalo, along with Antonio, Sebastian, Adrian, and Francisco. All stand in the charmed circle that Prospero has made.

Prospero reassures Gonzalo that surely as the morning drives away the night, the charms will dissolve, and the others will come to their senses. He praises Gonzalo for his loyalty and promises to reward him. He tries to remind Alonso of how he and Sebastian have wronged him. Prospero reminds his own brother, Antonio, of his too-great ambition and of his plotting with Sebastian to kill King Alonso. He then forgives them for their evil ways. Actually, Alonso, Sebastian, and Antonio have not returned to "normal" and do not recognize Prospero or understand him.

Prospero sends Ariel to get the hat and rapier (sword) that he wore when he was duke of Milan, wanting them to see him in familiar garments.

Ariel's next task is to go to the ship that was supposedly wrecked but that actually is anchored safely in one of the island's coves. He is to bring back the captain and the boatswain.

Good Gonzalo is amazed by the strange things that are happening. Prospero again talks directly to King Alonso. Presenting himself as the "wronged duke of Milan," he embraces the king, proving that he is indeed flesh and blood, not a spirit. He then welcomes the entire company.

Alonso, as amazed as his counselor, accepts that Prospero is alive, begs his pardon, and asks how he came to be in this place. Before answering him, Prospero embraces Gonzalo and repeats his welcome. In an aside to Antonio and Sebastian, he says that if he chose to tell the king of their plan, they would be punished as traitors, but he promises, "I will tell no tales."

Alonso asks again for details of what has taken place and speaks sadly of the loss of his son, Prince Ferdinand. Prospero does not tell him that Ferdinand is safe. Instead, he says that he has had a similar loss, his daughter, Miranda. Alonso says he wishes that he had been the one drowned and that his son and Prospero's daughter were back in Naples as its king and queen.

Still speaking in riddles, Prospero says that his daughter was lost in the storm which caused them temporarily to lose their senses. He says little more, other than that he lives on the island with a few attendants and that in return for Alonso's restoring his dukedom, he will repay the king with something that will "content" him.

Next, Prospero "discovers" Miranda and Ferdinand at a game of chess. Alonso can't believe that Ferdinand is real, and Sebastian calls it a miracle. Ferdinand says that although he cursed the seas, they have been merciful. Alonso blesses Ferdinand, then asks how he has come to the island and who the young woman is. (He thinks that she is a goddess.)

Miranda, seeing all the men, utters a speech that is often quoted:

(continued)

What Happens in Act V, *The Tempest* (continued)

How many goodly creatures are there here!
How beauteous mankind is! O brave new world,
That has such people in it!

Ferdinand explains to his father that Miranda, his beloved, is the daughter of the duke of Milan.

Alonso murmurs that he will have to ask his child's forgiveness, but Prospero tells him to forget the past.

Gonzalo asks the gods' blessing on the young couple. He believes it was all part of the gods' plan that Prospero was driven temporarily from his kingdom, only to have it restored and his daughter engaged to Ferdinand. They, the "shipwrecked," have had their lives restored.

Ariel reappears with the ship's captain and boatswain. Gonzalo asks how they survived. The boatswain has no explanation but says that their ship is as seaworthy as when they first set sail.

Alonso, certain that the things that have happened must have supernatural causes, also questions the boatswain. He says only that they slept, were awakened by strange noises, and found their ship in excellent shape. Alonso is still puzzled, but Prospero tells him not to worry. When they have time, Prospero will explain everything to him.

Prospero sends Ariel to get Caliban, Stephano, and Trinculo, first removing Prospero's spell. Ariel returns almost immediately with the three. Stephano says that they must "stick together." Trinculo is pleased to see the others from the "shipwreck." Caliban sees Prospero dressed as a duke, admires him, and hopes that Prospero won't scold him. Sebastian and Antonio, always cynical, wonder if the trio are marketable (could be sold as slaves). Prospero explains to Alonso that two of the men are Alonso's own retainers. The third "mis-shapen knave" belongs to Prospero himself.

Alonso and Sebastian, recognizing Stephano and Trinculo, wonder where they have found the wine that has made them drunk. Prospero taunts Stephano about his ambition to be king of the island. Stephano answers humbly that he would not have made a good one.

Alonso is fascinated by Caliban's strange appearance. Prospero says that bad manners match his bad appearance. He then sends Caliban to set the house in order and to return the garments that they have stolen.

If Caliban does a good job, Prospero says he may forgive him. Filled with guilt, Caliban scolds himself for having taken Stephano for his master.

Prospero invites the king and his followers to spend the night. He will then explain to Alonso all that has happened. He promises that in the morning their ship will be ready, and, with good winds to aid them, they will catch up with the rest of the fleet. He also says that he hopes Ferdinand and Miranda will marry. Then he will return to Milan.

Epilogue

Prospero returns to the stage alone to give the epilogue, or concluding speech. In it are echoes of his earlier speech in Act IV, Scene I, lines 148–158, "Our revels now are ended." He says that his time as a powerful sorcerer is over. "What strength I have's mine own, Which is most faint." He calls on some power (or powers) to help him return to Milan: "Gentle breath of yours my sails must fill." It is ironic that Prospero, who had Caliban, Ariel, and the other spirits to do his bidding, now calls upon a greater power than himself to free him— actually, to let him return to his former life.

Lesson 40: Master and Slave

For many readers, the contrast between master and slave in *The Tempest* is one of the most interesting parts of the play. On one level is Prospero, of high birth, rightful duke of Milan, learned, self-controlled, and, through his magic, able to manipulate or control the lives of others. Far below him in status is his slave, Caliban, the son of a sorceress, misshapen and ugly, and seemingly lacking in any moral sense (remember that he once tried to rape Miranda). At first reading, there seems to be nothing admirable about him. Yet a number of fine Shakespearean actors have chosen to play the role of Caliban. In this lesson, you will find out why. You will also determine whether or not Prospero's character is completely without flaws.

1. As an in-class exercise, think of adjectives other than those in the paragraph above that describe either Prospero or Caliban. One person should be designated to write two separate lists on the chalkboard.

2. Next, try to come up with an actual incident that demonstrates that each adjective you chose really fits the character. Where in the play does Prospero or Caliban show that he has this trait?

3. Did you think of any adjectives for Prospero that are not complimentary? For example, do you feel he is ever not mindful of his responsibilities? How about his treatment of Caliban? Why is he careful to praise Ariel for every task he completes? Does he ever praise Caliban?

   _____

4. How do you explain this treatment of Caliban? Do you think it is justified?

   _____

5. What did Caliban do for Prospero when he first arrived on the island? Caliban later promises to do the same thing for someone else (his new master). Who is it? Refer back to the text if you need to.

   _____

6. Do you think Caliban is observant? (*Hint:* What does he say is the source of Prospero's power?)

   _____

7. When Caliban, along with Stephano and Trinculo, is approaching Prospero's dwelling, why does he caution the others? What do you think this shows about him?

   _____

8. Does Caliban eventually realize that his judgment has been poor? Explain. (*Hint:* Remember that temporarily he has had a new master.)

   _____

9. Can you account for Caliban's unsocial behavior? (Remember his background, and consider the question in the light of present-day psychology.)

   _____

Reading Quiz: *The Tempest,* Act V

1. Among the people of high birth who were "shipwrecked," which one stands out for his goodness and loyalty?

   _____

2. How are the master of the ship and the boatswain awakened? (*Hint:* There is much noise. Who causes it?)

   _____

   _____

3. What is Miranda's reaction when she sees the "shipwreck" survivors for the first time?

   _____

   _____

4. Where will the king and his company spend their one night on the island?

   _____

5. What does Prospero hope his own future will be? _____

   _____

   _____

Name _____ Date _____

Final Test: *The Tempest*

Which of the adjectives in column 1 best describes each character in column 2? **Write the appropriate letter or letters in each space.**

Column 1

A. physically unattractive
B. innocent and loving
C. capable of magic
D. somewhat pathetic
E. power-hungry
F. ruthless
G. loyal
H. loving as a father
I. fond of drink
J. not qualified to lead
K. madly in love
L. home-educated
M. very intelligent
N. forgiving
O. reasonable

Column 2

1. Prospero _____
2. Miranda _____
3. Caliban _____
4. King Alonso _____
5. Gonzalo _____
6. Sebastian _____
7. Antonio _____
8. Ferdinand _____
9. Trinculo _____
10. Stephano _____

11. **Which of the following statements do you think summarizes the theme of the play?** Explain briefly.

   _____

   _____

   A. Power corrupts those who have it, and the desire for power may also corrupt.
   B. Evil-doers eventually receive the punishment they deserve.
   C. The play depicts ideal power and justice and how power can be used for good purposes.

12. **Who said it?**

   A. *O brave new world,*
      That has such people in it! _____

   B. *Our revels now are ended.* _____

   C. *We are such stuff as dreams are made on, and our little life*
      Is rounded with a sleep. _____

13. Shakespeare was a monarchist; that is, he believed that government by a good and just ruler was ideal. He also believed that if the rightful ruler was deposed or murdered, chaos would result.

   In this play, what rightful ruler is deposed? _____
   What happens then? _____

14. What is your reaction to Caliban? What do you think he represents?

   _____

   _____

15. *The Tempest* is a comedy, that is, in the end all is well. In a tragedy, on the other hand, the hero is usually destroyed. Does this play fit your idea of a comedy? Explain briefly.

   _____

   _____

Teacher's Ready Reference

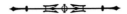

Romeo and Juliet

Lessons 1 and 2

(These lessons both require only that students outline what they have read.)

Lesson 3

Answer Key:

1. A. easily angered
   B. easily angered, hospitable
   C. lovesick, melancholy, handsome
   D. lighthearted
   E. sensible, peaceable
   F. hotheaded
   G. matter-of-fact
   H. talkative, bawdy
   I. wealthy, handsome
   J. beautiful
   K. just, peaceable
2. No, he is in love with love.
3. Benvolio says that if Rosaline won't have Romeo, he should find another girl.
4. She emphasizes that he is handsome and wealthy. She is shallow.
5. Yes. The serious quarrel between the Montagues and Capulets; Romeo's sense of dread about the Capulet party; Juliet's fear because she has fallen in love with an enemy.

Reading Quiz:

1. Both the servants and the prince comment on it.
2. Romeo avoided meeting Benvolio.
3. They are masked.
4. She praises Paris's appearance.
5. Twenty-five years ago, at least. Lady Capulet was about Juliet's age when Juliet was born, fourteen years ago.

Lesson 4

Answer Key:

1. She judges men, first of all, by appearance. She is fickle.
2. She is talkative and wanders from one topic to another.
3. She speaks to Juliet affectionately and is willing to help her love affair with Romeo.

4. Actually, she is deceiving the Capulets, who would not want Juliet to marry their enemy's son.
5. He treats the subject of love lightly. His long speech about Mab is imaginative. His explanation of dreams is both sound and well-expressed.
6. No, he treats the subject of love lightly.
7. He sees her as silly, vain, and self-important.
8. The earth produces all living things, but all living things die and return to the earth. Thus, the earth both gives and takes life.
9. Everything on earth has some worthwhile purpose.
10. He realized that Romeo's "love" for Rosaline would not be lasting. He hopes that Romeo's marriage to Juliet will bring peace to the Montagues and the Capulets.
11. Don't be too hasty. Think before you act.

Reading Quiz:

1. He says he has forgotten Rosaline.
2. They think Romeo has been up all night because he is lovesick for Rosaline.
3. She'd rather see a toad than Paris.
4. She enjoys her importance and Juliet's eagerness to hear the news. She claims she is tired.
5. Supposedly, she is going to confess her sins to Friar Lawrence.

Lesson 5

Answer Key:

1. Things are moving too quickly.
2. He speaks of being separated by death.
3. If Paris waits until Juliet is sixteen, and if Juliet herself consents to the match.
4. He wants the marriage to take place at once and assumes that Juliet will agree. He thinks marriage will end her grieving for Tybalt.
5. He no longer cares whether or not she wants to marry. He is angry that she opposes him because he thinks he is doing what is best for her.
6. He believes that the marriage may end the Montague-Capulet feud. He also thinks Romeo and Juliet are so wildly in love that they should

be married at once. She believes in love and wants Juliet to be happily married. Opinions will vary.

7. A. He chooses to attend the party.
   B. He fell in love by chance or fate.
   C. He chooses to marry Juliet.
   D. He is a victim of circumstance or fate.

Reading Quiz:

1. Tybalt takes advantage of Romeo when he tries to separate Tybalt and Mercutio.
2. the rope ladder
3. She is angry with Romeo.
4. Mantua
5. Romeo should stay in Mantua until tempers have cooled so that his marriage to Juliet can be announced and the prince's pardon obtained.
6. He is being "womanish."
7. She intends to have Romeo poisoned in Mantua.
8. commit suicide

Lesson 6

Answer Key:

1. When Juliet is his wife, she will be happy and happy to meet him. When Juliet can let it be known that she is Romeo's wife, then she will be happy.
2. First, the sweet sound (silver sound) of music; next, the pleasant sound of silver (money); next, musicians play for money (sound for silver); next, "silver sound" because musicians can expect only silver, not gold.
3. Answers will vary.
4. Answers will vary.
5. dictionary exercise
6. A. nuptial   D. beseeches
   B. disparagement   E. misadventure
   C. inconstant   F. fray

Reading Quiz:

Combined quiz for Lessons 6 and 7 appears after Lesson 7.

Lesson 7

Answer Key:

1. I'll gó/ alóng,/ no súch/ sight tó/ be shówn,

   But tó/ rejoíce/ in splén-/ dor óf/ mine ówn.

2. Mind to kingdom.
   It is a realm over which I have control.
3. She runs very fast.
4. He is very strong.
5. A. allusion
   B. simile
   C. metaphor

Reading Quiz:

1. forty-two hours
2. that Friar Lawrence might be poisoning her so no one will know that he performed a marriage for her and Romeo
3. He is quarantined.
4. warn his master of anyone's approach
5. leave at once and the next day carry a letter to Romeo's father
6. She died of grief for her son.
7. The Montague-Capulet feud is ended.

Lesson 8

Answer Key:

1. Answers will vary.
2. Answers will vary.
3. Answers will vary.
4. Answers will vary.

Final Test: *Romeo and Juliet*

1. Rosaline
2. Capulet party
3. were enemies
4. is quarantined and can't deliver the letter
5. Mercutio's, Tybalt's, banishment
6. death
7. any two of the following: the Prince, Benvolio, Friar Lawrence
8. Mercutio
9. Juliet's nurse
10. ending the feud, erecting statues to Romeo and Juliet's memory
11. Tybalt
12. take the potion that will put her into a coma
13. Tybalt, Paris
14. Romeo
15. Juliet
16. Friar Lawrence
17. Nurse
18. Answers will vary.
19. Answers will vary.

Julius Caesar

Lesson 9

Answer Key:

1. They dislike Caesar; the workingmen look up to him as their great hero.
2. Some are jealous of Caesar. Some fear that he is too ambitious and wants too much power.
3. A. Cassius
   B. Brutus
   C. by convincing Brutus that the people want him as their leader for the good of Rome
   D. Answers will vary.
4. Flavius and Marullus drive the workingmen from the street.
5. A. It troubles Caesar enough that he wants to see the man.
   B. Their conversation makes it clear that there is dissension, or disagreement. Not everyone admires Caesar.
   C. It shows him as physically vulnerable.
6. Answers will vary.

Lesson 10

Answer Key:

1. A. No, his answers to Marullus's questions have double meanings and thinly veiled humor.
   B. He puns cleverly and is more quick-witted than Flavius and Marullus.
2. A. Yes, he sees Cassius as too thoughtful, a potential troublemaker.
   B. Answers will vary.
   C. Caesar is epileptic and deaf in one ear. He did not have Cassius's stamina when they were swimming the Tiber.
3. A. Antony is to run the race that is part of the Lupercal celebration. Caesar mentions Antony's fondness for sports and music.
   B. Brutus sees himself as not "gamesome" and not eager for physical activities, as Antony is.
   C. He mentions Antony's fondness for games and music; Cassius, he says, reads and observes others, has no interest in sports, and smiles as if he doesn't mean it.
4. A. Caesar is frightened. Cassius, courageously, defies the storm and accuses Casca of weakness for not doing the same.

B. He compares threatening aspects of the storm to Caesar himself, although he does not openly name him.
C. He says that if Caesar becomes king, he will commit suicide. Casca vows that he could do that too, to escape bondage. Still, Cassius tests further, saying that maybe Casca is a willing bondman. Casca assures him that he is not.
D. Answers will vary.

Reading Quiz:

1. They plan to take the wreaths off statues of Caesar and drive other working people off the streets so that they won't be on hand to greet Caesar.
2. So she will conceive. She is childless.
3. Caesar tired, and Cassius had to carry him to shore.
4. He had a fever and a fit and was very weak.
5. his deafness and epilepsy
6. He will arrange to have Brutus receive many fictitious letters (supposedly from Roman citizens) urging Brutus to take action.
7. by suicide
8. He is highly respected and would lend his respectability to them.

Lesson 11

Answer Key:

1. His mind is troubled about what he believes is Caesar's ambition for power. He does not know what course to take, whether or not to join Cassius.
2. He must believe Caesar's death is for the good of Rome.
3. Answers will vary.
4. Caesar has more power than Cassius.
5. Cassius sees Antony as a shrewd schemer who may cause them trouble. Brutus sees Antony as harmless, unable to act without Caesar.
6. A. by flattery
   B. He is sneaky and unethical.
7. Answers will vary.
8. love and concern for their husbands
9. Portia seems Brutus's equal, a courageous, admirable woman. Calpurnia, not as strong a character, begs and coaxes her husband to win him to her way of thinking.
10. A. Cassius mentions Caesar's superstition. Caesar consults fortune-tellers.

B. He will not admit or give in to fear.

C. He says it is useless to fear death; he has the fatalism of a soldier.

D. Decius flatters him into going to the Senate House, saying this is the day he may be crowned.

E. He invites the conspirators to have wine before they start out for the Senate.

Reading Quiz:

1. He believes that once Caesar has absolute power, he will change and become a tyrant.
2. It has been in a state of insurrection; he does not know whether or not to act.
3. Cicero will not go along with others' plans; he likes to be in charge himself.
4. He sees Antony as harmless.
5. She gashes her thigh to show her courage.
6. They came in the night and hid their faces.
7. Antony

Lesson 12

Answer Key:

1. A. Whatever concerns him personally gets his attention last.
   B. Caesar is angered and thinks Artemidorus mad.
   C. He puts duty ahead of self but is somewhat arrogant.
2. A. He despises it and will not be swayed by it.
   B. He is constant; his mind cannot be changed.
   C. Answers will vary.
3. He sees the murder as a ritual killing for the good of Rome.
4. Answers will vary.
5. A. Answers will vary.
   B. It is logical that he might ask Caesar's forgiveness for joining with his killers. Most of the conspirators would trust him more, thinking that he was being honest, but Cassius has doubts.
6. Cassius was the better judge, for Antony is soon a dangerous force to be reckoned with.
7. He is sincere. He believes he acted for the good of Rome and puts Rome ahead of himself.
8. A. He reminds the people of all the selfless things Caesar did, not the acts of an ambitious man.
   B. He throws back the cloak so that the people can see Caesar's many wounds.
   C. For dramatic effect, so that the people will learn last that Caesar remembered them in his will.

Reading Quiz:

1. His addressing Caesar's corpse, begging forgiveness, makes Cassius suspicious.
2. He calls them butchers and swears revenge.
3. Caesar sent for him.
4. Caesar left a sum of money to each citizen and left his estate as a public park forever.
5. Octavius and Lepidus
6. They have ridden out of Rome in great haste.
7. The aroused mob looks only for a victim; thus, the innocent may suffer.

Lesson 13

Answer Key:

1. A. He is willing to condemn anyone, even his nephew. He scorns Lepidus and uses him.
   B. Answers will vary.
2. He breaks down and offers to let Brutus kill him, and he grieves when he hears of Portia's death. Obviously, his friendship for Brutus is genuine, and he craves Brutus's approval. He is not totally self-sufficient.
3. A. in talking of his wife's death
   B. toward the serving boy, Lucius
   C. toward Cassius, when Cassius says he will take no more insult
   D. in his contempt for Cassius's way of getting money, which Brutus would willingly have used to pay his troops
4. Self-righteousness
5. A. the purge of those whom the triumvirs distrust and, indirectly, Portia's death
   B. the civil war
6. Cassius and the conspirators; Antony. Deaths, often of the innocent.
7. Answers will vary.

Reading Quiz:

1. She swallowed hot coals.
2. seventy to a hundred
3. They will gain reinforcements.
4. that Brutus will see him at Philippi
5. whether or not to kill Antony and whether or not to let Antony address the crowd after Caesar's murder

Lesson 14

Answer Key:

1. In their first conversation, when he suggests that many in Rome would like Brutus as their ruler. He also suggests that Caesar has too much power and will gain more.
   Cassius respects Brutus and gives in to him.

2. The purge and civil war come as a result of Caesar's death.

3. Antony, by appealing to their emotions. They burn the conspirator's houses and kill an innocent man.

4. Answers will vary.

5. Antony, Octavius, and Lepidus's actions to destroy their enemies.

6. Brutus is willing to murder Caesar for the good of Rome; Cassius takes bribes to gain money to pay his troops and conduct war.

Reading Quiz:

1. The two eagles that follow his troops are replaced by birds that feed on carrion—ravens, kites, and crows.

2. He was being surrounded by friends.

3. He disappears.

4. It was his birthday.

5. He kills himself with Cassius's sword.

6. Caesar's ghost

7. He did what he thought was for the "common good of all." He was a gentle man.

Final Test: *Julius Caesar*

1. to help Rome

2. jealousy

3. men on fire in the streets, a lion in the street, terrible lightning

4. sacrifice, murder

5. speak to the crowd

6. A mob is dangerous.

7. convince him to go to the Senate House

8. bravery

9. Portia

10. his fall from power and his death

11. his not listening to those who tried to warn him

12. his troubled mind as he considers an awful deed

13. Cassius

14. Brutus

15. Caesar

16. Cassius

17. Brutus

18. Answers will vary.

Macbeth

Lesson 15

Answer Key:

1. Ross reports that everyone has sent messages to King Duncan, citing Macbeth's brave deeds, and that the king has rewarded Macbeth with the title of Thane of Cawdor.

2. Ross reports that the king both wonders at this bravery and praises his deeds. Of course, the king has also given him the new title.

3. Macbeth. He is so engrossed in his dreams and imaginings about the future that he pays scant attention to Ross and Angus.

4. Fears and imaginings already trouble him greatly.

5. Yes. He speaks of a horrid image that strikes fear to his heart.

6. They owe the king both service and loyalty. His feelings are probably mixed at that point. Later, after Duncan announces that Malcolm will succeed him, Macbeth considers murdering the king.

7. Duncan announces that Malcolm will succeed him.

8. He is too ambitious.

9. He wrote to Lady Macbeth about their promises.

10. He is ambitious, but not ruthless enough to gain what he wants by foul means. He has too much of "the milk of human kindness."

11. He confides in her; she understands him and is willing to use her strength to support him in areas where he may be weak. She wants whatever he wants. They do love each other and are happy to be reunited.

12. She is the stronger. She advises him as to what his behavior should be and tells him to leave the rest to her.

13. He speaks of the inevitable results of killing Duncan; the king is well liked; his death will cause consternation in Scotland. It is not the murder but its aftermath that causes Macbeth concern.

14. Yes. He knows his ambition is influencing him too much. He sees his crime as especially evil since he is killing his king. His king is also his guest, to whom every kindness should be done.

15. Answers will vary.

Reading Quiz:

1. by sending such winds against her husband's ship that he will not be able to make any progress

2. that he will beget kings

3. Prince of Cumberland
4. evil spirits
5. Any two: Macbeth is related to the king and is his subject; the king is his guest; the king's behavior has been so modest that he is loved by the people, and his death will cause consternation.
6. She will make his chamberlains drunk so that nothing will awaken them; thus, Duncan will be unguarded when she and Macbeth go to his room to kill him.

Lesson 16

Answer Key:

1. Answers will vary.
2. that he would like to receive what he wants legitimately, without doing anything wrong
3. She must spur him on when, because of his natural kindness, he is reluctant to act.
4. all remorse and gentleness; commit the murder
5. She tells him that his countenance (expression) is too open; people might read his thoughts; he must conceal them.
6. She greets the king warmly and assures him that his pleasure is her only concern.
7. No, but she thinks he is not ruthless enough to do what must be done to gain the throne. She must spur him on.
8. Answers will vary. She wants to shock him into doing the deed that earlier he had seemed more willing to do. She uses this method to strengthen his resolve.
9. Lady Macbeth
10. When she sees the king sleeping, he reminds her of her father, and she cannot kill him.
11. Answers will vary.

Lesson 17

Answer Key:

1. The place is lonely and bleak; the storm is threatening. Black.
2. Red. It is the symbol of the blood that has been shed on the battlefield.
3. Fog obscures. Nothing can be seen clearly. Macbeth and Banquo are not sure what they have seen, and they do not completely understand what they have been told. The fog covers the witches' disappearance effectively.
4. The raven is black, and black is a symbol for night and death. His voice is a harsh croak. He is associated, in superstition, with the powers of darkness.

5. The martin is a gentle, peaceable bird and a graceful, pretty bird, unlike the raven. Banquo's speech implies that where this bird nests, the air is "delicate" and the atmosphere harmonious; actually, Banquo and Duncan have come to a place of evil and death.
6. Duncan sees the castle and its surroundings as a place of calmness and peace. Of course, the readers know it as a place whose owners' minds are in a terrible turmoil and a place which will be the scene of Duncan's violent death.
7. Between midnight and dawn. Under cover of darkness, an evil deed was done.

Reading Quiz:

1. a diamond
2. They said their prayers and went back to sleep.
3. "Macbeth does murder sleep."
4. so that it will look as if they committed the murder
5. earthquakes, chimneys blown down, strange voices prophesying terrible things, and a bird crying all night
6. England and Ireland
7. He does not intend to go to the coronation.

Lesson 18

Answer Key:

1. He is very friendly to Banquo, seems to need his advice, and says he wants him as his honored guest for the banquet that night. Actually, he intends that Banquo be murdered before the banquet occurs.
2. Whether or not Fleance is going riding with his father. He wants to be sure that Fleance is killed too.
3. Yes. He mentions both Banquo's and Duncan's good qualities and admits that he has sold his soul to the devil because of ambition.
4. He convinces them that Banquo is the cause of their problems.
5. He does not tell her his plan to have Banquo and Fleance murdered.
6. He wants to spare her further concern and probably guilt.
7. He regrets aloud that Banquo is not with them, and he drinks to Banquo.
8. Banquo's ghost may be a figment of his imagination. He is convinced that "blood will have blood," that once set upon this course of evil, there is no turning back.
9. He has spies in various lords' houses and trusts no one.

10.   *For mine own good*
   All causes shall give way. I am in blood
   Stepp'd in so far that, should I wade no more,
   Returning were as tedious as go o'er.
   Strange things I have in head, that will to hand,
   Which must be acted e'er they may be scann'd.

Reading Quiz:

1. because he wants Fleance murdered too
2. deceived and double-crossed them
3. They are desperate, discouraged, and reckless
4. She suggests that they go home since any questioning of Macbeth will anger him.
5. He has spies in their household
6. Macduff does not attend the banquet although he has been invited.

Lesson 19

Answer Key:

1. modest and open in his dealings
2. A. consideration for an underling
   B. generous and appreciative
   C. concern for the welfare of Scotland
   D. gracious and appreciative
3. lustful, avaricious, selfish
   Answers will vary.
4. justice, verity, temperance, stableness, bounty, perseverance, mercy, lowliness, devotion, patience, courage, fortitude
5. He is a healer; praying over the ill and deformed, he cures them. He also has the gift of prophecy and is a most holy man.
6. He will repay those who have helped him. He will also give them the title of earl. He will call home those who were exiled during Macbeth's reign. He will punish those who carried out Macbeth's evil orders. In general, he will do what God guides him to do. Evidently, like his father, he will be kind and just, moving quickly and decisively to right wrongs and reward those who deserve reward.
7. When Duncan is murdered, Scotland is thrown into chaos. Evil reigns, in the person of Macbeth. The innocent (Banquo, Lady Macduff, and her children) suffer or are murdered. Only by civil war, which causes more bloodshed, is order restored.

Reading Quiz:

1. any three: toad, snake, eye of newt, toe of frog, wool of bat, tongue of dog, adder's tongue, blind-worm's sting, lizard's leg, owl's wing, scale of dragon, tooth of wolf, etc. (See Act IV, Scene I, lines 1–38.)

2. to kill Macduff
3. She is angry and feels her husband has deserted her.
4. any two: lustfulness, avarice, selfishness
5. his gift of healing

Lesson 20

Answer Key:

1. It makes it uneasy and spurs Macbeth to jealousy of Banquo. It makes Banquo suspicious of Macbeth and hopeful that the prophecy may come true for him as it has for Macbeth.
2. Eventually, it isolates him from her.
3. First he thinks it is a creation of his "heat-oppressed brain"; then he thinks it exists and that his eyes, not his other senses, may be right.
4. All nature seems dead, wicked dreams trouble sleepers, witchcraft prevails, murder stalks its victim, the very stones he walks on may "speak" of his evil intent.
5. Answers will vary.
6. his soul, the devil, murder
7. Macbeth is surprised and angry to hear Fleance has fled. Answers will vary.
8. Hallucination. They are uneasy. Uneasiness may lead to suspicion since Macbeth has behaved so strangely.
9. The apparition of the eight kings with Banquo following. The bloody child and the crowned child with the tree. They make him feel invincible since "none of woman born can harm Macbeth" and Birnam Wood, he thinks, cannot come to Dunsinane. Still, the apparition of the kings troubles him greatly.
10. Answers will vary.

Lesson 21

Answer Key:

1. Macbeth becomes increasingly ruthless; gradually, Lady Macbeth becomes conscience-stricken.
2. Banquo has been murdered; Macduff has lost his entire family.
3. People lived in fear; peace was destroyed.
4. Obviously, Malcolm is going to restore order.
5. The more evil things Macbeth does, the more he is willing to do to maintain his position.
6. Once he begins, he feels there is no turning back, and he has sold his soul to the devil.
7. It makes him willing to use any means to hold his position of power.
8. Answers will vary.

Lesson 22

Answer Key:

1. Awáy,/and márk/the tíme/with faír-/est shów . . .
2. Answers will vary.
3. Answers will vary.
4. brief candle, walking shadow, poor player, tale told by an idiot. No.
5. Answers will vary.
6. His virtues will plead like angels.
   Pity, like a naked new-born babe . . . or Heaven's cherubim.

Reading Quiz:

1. blood
2. that no man born of woman shall have power over Macbeth and that he need not fear until Birnam Wood shall come to Dunsinane
3. As they march forward, carrying the branches before them, it looks as if the forest is moving.
4. If his troops had not deserted to Malcolm's, he would have gone forward.
5. He will not strike at hired soldiers.
6. He was delivered by Caesarean section.
7. She commits suicide.

Final Test: *Macbeth*

1. Thane of Cawdor, king
2. beget kings
3. become remorseless and kill Duncan
4. Malcolm
5. sleep
6. They fear the murderer may strike them next.
7. him crowned
8. traitor
9. Malcolm orders his troops to cut branches to carry for camouflage
10. born not in the usual way, but by Caesarean section
11. Macduff
12. great ambition
13. Answers will vary.
14. Macbeth
15. Lady Macbeth
16. Macduff
17. Malcolm
18. Lady Macbeth
19. late, after midnight
20. Macbeth's
21. Far from being peaceful, as the description implies, it is the scene of murder.

Hamlet

Lesson 23

Answer Key:

1. He trembles and gets pale when he sees it; afterwards, he expresses the superstition that spirits have to disappear when the cock crows to signal dawn.
2. He crosses the ghost's path; that was considered very dangerous.
3. He sends Cornelius and Voltimand to Norway to try for a peaceful settlement. He takes care of Laertes' request quickly.
4. He thinks Hamlet is accepting his mother's second marriage.
5. He is disillusioned with his mother to the point of considering suicide.
6. They may not be completely honorable and think Hamlet's behavior would be like their own.
7. He doesn't care whether he lives or dies, and the spirit cannot harm his immortal soul.
8. to gain time to verify the ghost's accusation and protect himself in case Claudius has designs against him
9. He regrets that he is the one who must set matters right (take revenge). Answers will vary.
10. Answers will vary.

Reading Quiz:

1. It was believed that with the cock's crow, ghosts had to disappear.
2. that there has been some foul play
3. to tell no one else what has happened
4. A. to dress in expensive clothes, but not showy clothes
   B. To trusted old friends, do whatever you can to keep the friendship, but don't be too hasty in making new friends.
5. excessive drinking
6. by pouring poison into his ear while he is asleep
7. The ghost (beneath the floor) is echoing his words.

Lesson 24

Answer Key:

1. Polonius is suspicious by nature.
2. Answers will vary.
3. He suspects that something more than grief may be bothering Hamlet, and he wants to know what it is.
4. Queen Gertrude. Answers will vary.
5. Answers will vary.
6. His maintaining a good relationship with the king. When he hears of Hamlet's strange behavior in front of Ophelia, his first reaction is that Claudius must be told. He also is willing to use Ophelia as a decoy to find out what Hamlet is thinking.
7. because of his grief and disillusionment
8. He will use it as a trap to see if he can catch Claudius (prove his guilt).
9. He is a man who acts only after careful consideration; he accepts the possibility that the spirit he has seen is not his father's ghost, but an evil spirit tempting him to commit murder.

Reading Quiz:

1. money
2. his father's death and her remarriage
3. He will consider it.
4. She tells him to come to the point.
5. They have had strong competition from the boy actors.
6. He has not been able to bring himself to take action against Claudius.

Lesson 25

Answer Key:

1. He has assured Hamlet that he will inherit the throne. His manner to Hamlet is very kind, and he is pleased when Hamlet agrees to stay at court. He realizes how important Hamlet is to Gertrude, and, of course, he would like to have Hamlet, who is popular in Denmark, as an ally.
2. Polonius's comment about putting on a false face to hide evil within makes Claudius feel guilty. It is his conscience that affects him when he sees the play. Alone, he wants to pray for forgiveness and realizes that he cannot, since he has kept all the things he murdered for.
3. He knows Hamlet is not just lovesick, that Hamlet is not mad, and that whatever is troubling him makes him a threat.
4. He wants Horatio's objective reaction to Claudius's behavior at the play.

5. She does not know that Claudius has poisoned King Hamlet.
6. Guildenstern admits that he cannot play this little instrument, but he thinks he is clever enough to "sound" Hamlet and know what he is thinking. Hamlet takes that as an insult. Her understands immediately what Rosencrantz and Guildenstern are trying to do.
7. He tells himself that he must not do bodily harm to his mother.
8. It will be to their advantage with Claudius. Yes; their motive is self-advancement.
9. Since he assumes that Claudius is asking forgiveness for his sins, he fears that Claudius's soul might go to Heaven. Claudius has poisoned Hamlet's father (asleep) with all his sins upon his soul.
10. He sees him as a meddling old fool who got what he deserved.
11. He realizes she knew nothing about her husband's murder, and he trusts her enough to reveal his distrust of Rosencrantz and Guildenstern. He treats her more kindly.
12. He compares them to adders (snakes) who will try to sting him.

Reading Quiz:

1. She tells Ophelia that she hopes the cause of Hamlet's behavior is lovesickness for her and that Ophelia will bring him back to normal.
2. to a nunnery
3. Speak clearly, do not overact, but "suit action to the word."
4. She thinks the queen overdoes her profession of undying love.
5. that he lacks "advancement"—in other words, that he is not willing to wait to inherit the throne
6. He calls Polonius an "intruding fool" and indicates that he thought he was killing Polonius's "better" (Claudius).

Lesson 26

Answer Key:

1. She says that in his madness, Hamlet killed Polonius. She reveals nothing else.
2. Answers will vary.
3. She tries to calm Laertes and defends Claudius. She loves Claudius.
4. She feels very guilty and fears she shows it. She fears something terrible is about to occur.
5. They are out of place coming from this innocent girl and show how greatly her mind is deranged.

6. Yes. Answers will vary.
7. It is only after the play that Claudius is certain that Hamlet is his enemy. Even then, in getting rid of Hamlet (sending him to England), he acts in a way that would not offend the people of Denmark. Of course, since Gertrude doesn't know his whole plan, he will not offend her. Therefore, his reasons for not acting before are honest.
8. It is not playing by the rules. They take advantage of Hamlet's being honorable and, therefore, expecting no trick. Laertes, a good swordsman, should be willing to face Hamlet in a fair fight.
9. He cries for his sister, but at the same time, vows vengeance, which he will get by dishonest means.

Reading Quiz:

1. under the stairs going to the lobby
2. Horatio
3. They are very excited and want to forcibly enter the room where Claudius is.
4. fencing
5. She tries to hang some flowers in the branches of a willow but falls into the stream; her clothes become soaking wet, and she sinks.
6. He says he was trying to calm Laertes' rage.

Lesson 27

Answer Key:

1. Comic relief. They have become somewhat hardened to their job. Also, they joke to keep up their own spirits.
2. No matter what status we achieve in this life, it is soon forgotten. All are equal in the grave.
3. because she took her own life
4. He is silly and insincere. Answers will vary.
5. He is interested in self-preservation above all.
6. If he had a chance to be king, he would have been "most royal." He should have a hero's burial.

Reading Quiz:

1. because she is a gentlewoman
2. humor, puns
3. that Ophelia would become Hamlet's wife
4. They are amused by him and his pretentious language. They are also scornful of him.
5. when the English ambassador tells Fortinbras
6. his death
7. Being "most royal," he is concerned for the welfare of his country and wants an orderly succession.

Lesson 28

Answer Key:

1. Both Horatio and Hamlet accept the idea that ghosts exist and accept the popular beliefs about them.
2. Because he has died without confessing his sins, doing penance, and receiving absolution.
3. They held a subordinate position, accepting the authority of father, brother, and, finally, husband.
4. If one's spouse died, it was wrong to marry a close relative of the spouse. (For example, Henry VIII had to obtain permission from the pope to marry his elder brother Arthur's widow, Katherine of Aragon. Later, Henry wanted to have his marriage declared illegal, despite the permission.)
5. With King Hamlet's death, all of Denmark suffered. Answers will vary.
6. competition from the boy actors
7. Suicide was considered a sin.
8. Answers will vary. (Basically, that the mentally ill should be confined for the general good.)
9. Presentations may have been overly dramatic, with the actors shouting too loudly and taking liberties with the script, adding lines to get a laugh from the audience. Shakespeare preferred a more natural style of acting. Hamlet also emphasizes that the actors should speak clearly.
10. the divine right of kings

Lesson 29

Answer Key:

1. elegant language, extravagant praise, poetry, assurances of eternal devotion
2. The clown has just used *lie* in the sense of rest (in the grave). Hamlet uses *lie* as in *tell a lie*.
3. As time passes, love, which in the beginning is very strong, gradually lessens in intensity. It is as if love carries within itself the seed of its destruction (abatement).
4. Answers will vary.

Lesson 30

Answer Key:

1. I stáy/too lóng./But heŕe/my fá-/ther comés.
2. dictionary exercise
3. **Metaphor:**
   What a piece of work is man!
   Man—the beauty of the world

Man—the paragon of animals
Man—this quintessence of dust
Simile:
Man—in action how like an angel
Man—in apprehension how like a god

4. Answers will vary.

Final Test: *Hamlet*

1. tell the Norwegian king that his nephew is threatening Denmark
2. she has remarried so soon after his father's death—and to a man whom Hamlet considers to be far inferior to his father
3. they believe that he is only toying with her affections
4. take revenge
5. gain time to collect evidence against his uncle and to protect himself while he is doing it
6. spy on Laertes
7. spy on Hamlet and to sound him out to see what is bothering him
8. having the players perform a play in which the murder parallels the one Claudius committed
9. he has not given up the kingdom and the queen, both gained by the murder
10. death
11. murdered, are murdered
12. her father's death, Hamlet's rejection of her, and his "madness"
13. she commits suicide
14. death
15. Hamlet
16. Hamlet
17. Claudius
18. Gertrude
19. Hamlet
20. Fortinbras
21. Answers will vary.

A Midsummer Night's Dream

Lesson 31

Answer Key:

1. It is four days until the wedding. The time will go quickly. They will have a new moon.
2. How is Hermia to be punished if she continues to disobey Egeus?
3. He professed love earlier to Helena.
4. They will flee to his aunt's house outside Athens and be married there.
5. She talks about it enviously.
6. It is a tragedy.

Reading Quiz:

1. a new moon
2. She will be forced to enter a nunnery or die.
3. He mentions Demetrius's earlier affair with Helena.
4. Demetrius's love
5. Bottom

Lesson 32

Answer Key:

1. Oberon wants the mortal child that Titania has as her page.
2. fogs, floods, rotted crops, animals dead of disease, humans ill, seasons altered
3. Cupid's arrow missed its mark and fell upon the little flower.
4. He wants Demetrius to fall in love with Helena again.
5. Sprinkles Lysander's eyelids. Lysander sees and falls in love with Helena.
6. Helena still loves Demetrius. Lysander loves her. Demetrius loves Hermia. Hermia feels forsaken.

Reading Quiz:

1. Queen Elizabeth I
2. They are guards or soldiers for Queen Elizabeth.
3. Answers will vary. No.
4. Circle the world in forty minutes.
5. It will serve as a garment for a fairy.

Lesson 33

Answer Key:

1. Quince, chose the play, will arrange for props.
2. Bottom
3. How will he learn his lines? He has no talent.
4. Answers will vary.
5. He makes appropriate jokes with the fairies. Lines 182–201, Act III, Scene I.
6. Answers will vary. Possibilities: Titania—considerate; Oberon—determined; Puck—mischievous
7. Hermia. Helena. Answers will vary.

Reading Quiz:
1. Helena, Helena, Demetrius, Lysander
2. Fairies who take care of Bottom
3. He doesn't have to flee at daylight, for he is a different kind of spirit.
4. She thinks he is just mocking her.
5. Hermia thinks that Helena has stolen Lysander. Helena thinks that Hermia is part of the plot to mock her.

Lesson 34

Answer Key:
1. Oberon, Titania's
2. Quince, the artisan-actors
3. Titania, her attendants, Bottom
4. Puck, just before dawn

Reading Quiz:
1. Answers will vary.
2. Answers will vary.
3. Answers will vary.
4. Answers will vary.
   Possibilities: **Puck**: cynical, mischievous **Oberon**: basically kind, somewhat vengeful **Titania**: not easily influenced, concerned for others

Lesson 35

Answer Key:
1. Answers will vary.
2. Answers will vary.
3. Answers will vary.
4. The poet, frenzied, looks everywhere, up and down.

5. Answers will vary.
6. Answers will vary.
7. Answers will vary.

Reading Quiz:
1. Theseus
2. Hippolyta
3. Rustic dance
4. Puck, around midnight
5. He believes that Thisby is dead.

Final Test: *A Midsummer Night's Dream*
1. Theseus: D, L
2. Hippolyta: M
3. Lysander: E
4. Hermia: H
5. Demetrius: F
6. Helena: I
7. Egeus: C
8. Bottom: J
9. Quince: G
10. Oberon: A
11. Titania: B
12. Puck: K, N
13. Lysander
14. Puck
15. Queen Elizabeth I
16. Because Oberon wants the mortal child that Titania has as her page
17. Sent to a nunnery or put to death
18. Don't eat garlic or onions; your breath might offend the audience.
19. Answers will vary.
20. Answers will vary.

The Tempest

Lesson 36

Answer Key:
1. A. *Hamlet*
   B. *Romeo and Juliet*
   C. *A Midsummer Night's Dream*
2. Answers will vary, but Prospero did not carry out his responsibilities.
3. He is generous.
4. Answers will vary.
5. Answers will vary, possibly brutish.
6. Answers will vary.
7. Answers will vary.

Reading Quiz:
1. a shipwreck
2. patronizing, disrespectful
3. Gonzalo had put Prospero's own books into the boat with him so that he could teach Miranda.
4. No. He thinks his father is dead, but he is not.
5. Caliban

Lesson 37
Answer Key:
1. **Trinculo**: opportunistic, practical
   Caliban: servile, starved for kindness, generous, humble

Stephano: opportunistic, ingenious

2. He gave Caliban a drink of wine.
3. He thinks he can sell Caliban as a curiosity.
4. No. He thinks he and Trinculo will gain power.
5. Stephano
6. Caliban. He will steal from his master when no one is looking.

Reading Quiz:

1. No.
2. No.
3. His own position will be stronger with Sebastian, the king of Naples, indebted to him.
4. Ariel
5. They say they have heard a noise and have drawn their swords to protect Alonso.
6. He also thinks he has heard a humming noise.

Lesson 38

Answer Key:

1. No, he turned over his responsibilities to Antonio.
2. strengthen his own position
3. Ariel. Harshly. He praises Ariel and is critical of Caliban. Prospero's too demanding.
4. He will kill Gonzalo, and Antonio will kill Alonso. If Sebastian is king and indebted to Antonio, Antonio will expect many favors.
5. Prospero is harsh to him. He doesn't seek power.
6. Gonzalo

Reading Quiz:

1. books
2. Antonio, Sebastian, Alonso
3. loyalty
4. No, he thinks Ferdinand has drowned.
5. He is misshapen.

Lesson 39

Answer Key:

1. Answers will vary.
2. Answers will vary.
3. Answers will vary.
4. The world. All will disappear. Answers will vary.
5. Answers will vary.

Reading Quiz:

1. Their wine.
2. He thinks it is but trash. He is not interested in material things.

3. He praises Ariel but criticizes Caliban.
4. He tells him that he must not make love to Miranda before they are married.
5. the nymphs and the reapers' dance

Lesson 40

Answer Key:

1. in class exercise
2. in class exercise
3. Answers will vary.
4. Answers will vary.
5. He showed him where to get water and food. Stephano
6. Answers will vary, but it should be *yes*.
7. He wants to take Prospero by surprise. He thinks ahead more than the other two.
8. Yes. He sees Stephano as a mere drunkard, not worthy to be a master.
9. Possible answer: His mother was a witch. He has been alone with no socializing influences.

Reading Quiz:

1. Gonzalo
2. Ariel
3. She thinks they are beautiful and wonderful.
4. with Prospero
5. that he will return as duke to Milan

Final Test: *The Tempest*

1. C, H, M, N, O
2. B, K, L
3. A, D
4. E, F, H
5. G, O
6. E, F
7. E, F
8. K
9. I
10. E, I, J
11. Answers will vary.
12. A. Miranda
    B. Prospero
    C. Prospero
13. Prospero. Milan comes under the influence of Naples. Ruthless people plan murders to gain more power.
14. Answers will vary.
15. Answers will vary.